How Does a Typical Day Begin in Your House?

Do you spend twenty minutes trying to get your youngsters up and ready for school while your three-year-old throws a tantrum?

Do your kids refuse breakfast, hassle you about the clothes you've set out for them, then complain about the lunches you're packing?

Have you lost control before the day even begins?

Dr. Leman's action-oriented method puts you back in command. He shows you:

- How children learn
- How to be the authority in your home without being authoritarian
- Why reward and punishment no longer work
- Why—and how—reality discipline does

Filled with real-life incidents and familiar anecdotes, here is real, practical help and freedom from confusion. Start using reality to teach your children on a day-to-day basis. Begin to make your children mind lovingly, wisely, and well.

Making Children Mind
without Losing Yours

Books by Dr. Kevin Leman

Becoming the Parent God Wants You to Be
Becoming a Couple of Promise
Women Who Try Too Hard
When Your Best Is Not Good Enough
Winning the Rat Race without Becoming a Rat
Living in a Stepfamily without Getting Stepped On
Unlocking the Secrets of Your Childhood Memories
Growing Up Firstborn
Keeping Your Family Together When the World Is Falling Apart
Bringing Up Kids without Tearing Them Down
The New Birth Order Book
Sex Begins in the Kitchen
The Six Stress Points in a Woman's Life
What a Difference a Daddy Makes

Video Series

Bringing Up Kids without Tearing Them Down
Keeping the Promise
Parenting by Heart

Making Children Mind without Losing Yours

Dr. Kevin Leman

Fleming H. Revell
A Division of Baker Book House Co
Grand Rapids, Michigan 49516

© 1984, 2000 by Dr. Kevin Leman

Published by Fleming H. Revell
a division of Baker Book House Company
P.O. Box 6287, Grand Rapids, MI 49516-6287

Eleventh printing, April 2004

Printed in the United States of America

Library of Congress Cataloging-in-Publication Data

Leman, Kevin.
    Making children mind without losing yours / Kevin Leman.—2nd ed.
      p.   cm.
    ISBN 0-8007-5731-9 (pbk.)
    1. Discipline of children. 2. Child rearing. 3. Parenting—Religious aspects—Christianity. I. Title.

HQ770.4.L44 2000
649'.64—dc21   00-037280

Unless otherwise indicated, Scripture quotations are from *The Living Bible* © 1971. Used by permission of Tyndale House Publishers, Inc., Wheaton, IL 60189. All rights reserved.

Scripture quotations identified KJV are from the King James Version of the Bible.

Scripture quotations identified NIV are from the HOLY BIBLE, NEW INTERNATIONAL VERSION®. NIV®. Copyright © 1973, 1978, 1984 by International Bible Society. Used by permission of Zondervan Publishing House. All rights reserved.

Quotations from *God, the Rod, and Your Child's Bod* by Larry Tomczak. Copyright © 1981, 1982 by Larry and Doris Tomczak, published by Fleming H. Revell Company. Used by permission.

For current information about all releases from Baker Book House, visit our web site:
http://www.bakerbooks.com

To Kristin Leman O'Reilly,

our middle child and second daughter,
who endured many hand-me-downs
and far fewer pictures in the family photo album.
Your contagious smile, your sensitivity to others,
and your love for God make me proud to be your daddy.
May you enjoy this book when rearing your own little
ankle biters! You'll do a great job.
I love you, Krissy. God bless you.

Contents

PART 1

Why Reality Discipline Will Work in Your Home

One

It's a Jungle Out There!
Grab a Vine

Raising a child these days can be very scary.

In horror I watched the reports of the shooting spree in Littleton, Colorado, where teenagers were gunned down in their own high school. A few months later, a shooter invaded a preschool in Southern California. These incidents grabbed headlines, but in many urban areas drive-by shootings are too commonplace to get much press. Everywhere, children are at risk. And who knows what tragedies the new millennium will hold?

But it's not just bullets I'm worried about. Kids are being held hostage by coarse TV shows, violent video games, and valueless schools. Can they come through all of that with sweet spirits and strong morals, with self-confidence and concern for others? Is it possible to bring up good children in such a crazy age?

Sure, it's possible. But it's still scary.

Many parents I know worry that *they* are the danger, that somehow they'll do something terribly wrong, warping their children for life. They fear that they'll be too demanding or too permissive, too clinging or too distant. They end up paralyzed in their parenting, unable to help their children grow because they're too afraid to do anything.

I remember how petrified I was when I held my first child. She was a bundle of joy but I cradled her like fine china, fearing that I'd hurt her. And the fact is, in the twenty-seven years since then I *did* make mistakes, and so did my wife. I'm sure we hurt little Holly in certain ways, but we also helped her grow. Now she's a beautiful young lady, newly married, the head of a high school English department. Whew! We made it!

Of course we can't take too much of a breather—there are four other little Lemans right behind her. At this writing, our youngest is seven, so we're still in the thick of the parenting business. And it's still scary, especially as we see the world changing around us.

But I've got great news for you: You are going to make mistakes in parenting just as Sande and Kevin Leman did—guaranteed! You may not make the *same* mistakes, but you'll make plenty. I still remember one day when my eleven-year-old daughter looked up at me angrily and said, "You know what you ought to do? *Read your own book!*" Mistakes are part of the journey called parenting. But the good news is that you can learn from them. You can improve your parenting, building responsible kids and building joyful relationships with them.

Hillary Rodham Clinton took the title for her book from an old proverb: "It takes a village to raise a child." The saying makes some sense, I guess—we can all use others' help in caring for our kids. But the problem is, it's not a village, Hillary. It's a jungle out there. We're just swinging through, grabbing vine after vine, holding on for dear life. And we don't need the community to raise our kids, we don't need the schools to do it, we don't need the government telling us how, we don't even need churches to do our child rearing for us . . . we need *parents* to step up and do it. And we need everyone else—community, school, government, church—to support the parents in their efforts.

That's my challenge to you. Step up to the plate and be a parent. Decide that your family is your most important calling and commit yourself to it. Take the job of caring for your kids. It won't be easy. It won't always be fun. But it will be worth it.

You'll never be a perfect parent. You don't even have to be a great parent. But I'm urging you to take the time and effort to be a good parent. You can do it. This book can help.

An Idea Whose Time Has Come

The time has come for an idea I call reality discipline. It's a consistent, decisive, and respectful way for parents to love and discipline their children. (Notice I said "discipline" and not "punish." I said "love" and not "smother love.") Reality discipline steers a course between an authoritarian style and a permissive style, giving kids some choices but also holding them accountable.

I'm as happy as anyone that we no longer live in the Dark Ages when children were supposed to be seen and not heard and heaven help them if they let out a peep. I'm also relieved to see that we no longer wallow in the overpermissiveness of the 1950s and 1960s, which saw many parents being led astray by the notion that disciplining their children would inhibit their little psyches.

Now I see many families groping between those two extremes. As a family therapist, I talk to parents and their children every week. I also travel widely to speak to parents and teachers about child-rearing, discipline, and guidance. What I see and hear is that, in too many homes today, otherwise sophisticated and educated parents are still not sure they know the difference between discipline and punishment, between permissiveness and loving nurture. They're asking questions like:

How do I really love my children?

How do I respect my children?

How can I hold them accountable for their actions?

How do I get them to do what I think they ought to do, without resorting to physical or verbal violence?

What about spanking? Is it necessary? How much? How often?

In this book I present "reality discipline." It's an attempt to answer all those questions in a sensible, workable way.

Once I was flying home from appearing on "The 700 Club" when a businessman across the aisle struck up a conversation with me. Now I'm not a talker on airplanes, but this man was. After he rambled on for a while, he asked, "And what do you do?"

I'm always hesitant to say I'm a psychologist or a Christian speaker—both of those tend to spook people. So I said, "I was just doing a show."

He asked more about it, and I described the family building comments I had presented on the TV program.

"That is really good stuff," he said. "Where did a young man like you get such wisdom?" (At least I was younger than he was.)

"To tell you the truth," I replied, "I got it out of one book." He immediately reached into his pocket and pulled out a little computer with a notepad program, preparing to write the title and author of this brilliant book.

"It's the *Bible*," I said slowly. "B-I-B-L-E."

The truth is that reality discipline is inspired by Scripture. It actually finds its basis in a brief passage from the New Testament where the apostle Paul writes:

Children, obey your parents; this is the right thing to do because God has placed them in authority over you. Honor your father and mother. This is the first of God's Ten Commandments that ends with a promise. And this is the promise: that if you honor your father and mother, yours will be a long life, full of blessing.

And now a word to you parents. Don't keep on scolding and nagging your children, making them angry and resentful. Rather, bring them up with the loving discipline the Lord himself approves, with suggestions and godly advice.

Ephesians 6:1–4

The words I want to pay particular attention to are *obey, authority,* and *loving discipline.* My goal is to give parents specific ways to use their authority correctly as they bring up obedient children with loving discipline.

At this point you may be trying to place me on some kind of scale. How firm do I believe a parent should be? Do I recommend spanking or not? Well, I believe spanking has a place, but in most cases it should not take first place. At the same time, I strongly believe that when we discipline children, their psyches are not in danger. The white-glove technique went out with the early excesses of Dr. Spock.

But the keynote of reality discipline is *love.* One of the astounding things that I see again and again is that many children don't feel loved in their own homes. Family counselor Craig Massey conducted a survey of 2,200 teenagers from Christian homes across the United States. A startling 79 percent claimed they felt a lack of love at home. For discipline to work, the first thing that must happen is that the child must feel genuinely loved. Built on this loving foundation, reality discipline uses guidance and action-oriented techniques that force a child to accept responsibility and learn accountability for his or her actions.

Seven Principles of Reality Discipline

I hesitate to offer a set number of "steps" or "secrets" of reality discipline, because it's never that easy. It's often a matter of trial and error. You develop a feel for it. The rest of this book discusses the details of applying this child-rearing method, and it's hard to condense it all into a few catchphrases. But with all of that in mind, let me give you seven "principles" on which reality discipline is based.

1. Establish a healthy authority over your children.

A family is not a democracy. The parents need to be in charge. As Ephesians 6 says, God has placed parents in authority over children. So it's not just your own authority you're establishing, but God's.

If we make kids the centerpiece of the family, we teach them that they're the center of the universe, that their happiness reigns supreme. Nothing could be further from the truth. Too many pampered kids get out into the world and are shocked that the world does *not* revolve around them. They're princes and princesses at home but peons in real life, and they can't handle it. The best preparation for the real world is a home in which the children are valued family members—but not the be-all and end-all.

Kids need parents to be parents. They *want* parents to be parents. Their displays of power and rebellion are tests of your willingness to parent them. If you don't establish your parental authority, no one else will. Not the schools, not the media, certainly not their peers. Don't be afraid to take charge in your home. What you say goes.

But your authority must be a healthy one. In light of Ephesians 6:4, you can't be "scolding and nagging your children, making them angry and resentful." Your authority needs to be a display of love more than power.

2. Hold your children accountable for their actions.

As parents we're all home-schoolers. We should be teaching our kids every day that there are consequences for their actions, some positive and some negative. That's one of the most important things they'll ever learn.

"Write me a note, I'm late," your daughter says on the way to the car.

"What should I write?" you ask innocently. "That Ashley was late today because . . . why?"

"I need a note!" she pleads, beginning to worry that you won't bail her out this time.

"Well, I have to tell the truth," you respond. "So what should I say? She's late because she was on the phone with her girlfriend for twenty minutes when she should have been getting ready for school. Please do whatever you do to kids who are late for no good reason."

"Mom!"

Ashley thinks you're the grinch who stole Christmas, but you're actually giving her a great gift. You're showing her that her actions matter. You're refusing to bail her out of a mess she got into. If you make excuses for her, you're just letting her continue her irresponsible behavior. But no, you're respecting her choices enough to let her face the consequences. You're holding her accountable for her actions.

3. Let reality be the teacher.

When a cat runs into the street when a car's coming, it becomes a flat cat. We're all sad about that, but the reality is that if it had stopped and looked both ways, it would still be alive. That's a valuable lesson children can learn through observation or through experience.

That's why I love goldfish as pets. If you don't feed them, they die. Children learn that they must care for creatures and things in their care, or else they lose them. You can't resuscitate a dead goldfish. You can't undo that death, no matter how much you want to. Your children may be very sad about it, but that's how they learn. (The fact is, even when you care properly for goldfish, sometimes they die. This can also give you an opportunity to teach your kids about the realities of life and death.)

Look for teachable moments when you can use reality to deliver a powerful lesson. Maybe you let your kids stay up late one night just to show them how tired they'll feel the next day. (But then it's your responsibility to enforce a reasonable bedtime.)

Don't be afraid to let your kids fail. Too many parents worry that failure will scar their children's self-esteem. As a result the parents cheat, change the rules, pretend the child didn't fail, or keep the child from trying anything new. They feel guilty for not protecting their youngsters from such failure, and that guilt propels all sorts of bad decisions. (Visit the science fair at your child's school. Can you pick out the two or three projects that were actually done by the students themselves?)

Your home needs to be a place where your kids can fail—and learn from their failure. Surround them with love, show them how important they are to you, but don't try to undo their failures. It's not our job as parents to get our kids off the hook. Our job is to keep them on the hook. Reality is a great teacher, and if you teach children to learn from reality, its lessons will continue through their whole lives.

4. Use action more than words.

Your children already know what you're going to say. Half the time they can say it *for* you. "Don't be late, you're going to miss the bus." "Careful, you're going to poke your eye out!" "I'm not going to say this again . . ." But of course you *do* say it again . . . and again . . . and again.

We're tempted to try to teach with words. "I'll let you go this time, but don't let it happen again." Which do you think speaks louder—the words *don't let it happen again* or the action of letting them go this time? The action wins out every time.

When my son, Kevin, was in eighth grade, he asked me for help preparing for a spelling test at school. Normally I'd be glad to help him, but it was 10 p.m., and he had just spent two hours watching TV. I said no, explaining that he should have put his studies first. It was too late now.

You might think that's harsh. I suppose I could have wagged my finger at him, saying, "All right, but next time I won't be so nice." Those words wouldn't have meant anything, but my actions taught him some responsibility. And wouldn't you know it? I heard him shuffling in his room early the next morning, studying for that test.

With reality discipline, you need to state your expectations clearly. Let your children know their responsibilities to the family, to the school, to others. But then you don't need to keep repeating yourself. Let your actions speak for you.

5. Stick to your guns, but don't shoot yourself in the foot.

Kids are marathon runners, members of the ankle-biter battalion. They know that if they just keep whining, keep pleading, keep arguing, they can wear you down and get their way. You have to outlast them. They'll come up with a million reasons why your discipline is "just not fair!" But you're the boss. You've made a decision, so stick with it. Granted, your decisions won't always have the wisdom of Solomon, but you need to teach your kids that what you say goes. Give in, and they'll whine even more next time. Outlast them, and they'll learn that it's pointless to whine.

There are some exceptions. Remember that even your authority is not the ultimate—God's authority is. So if you're getting the idea that a different decision would be wiser or fairer, you can change your mind.

I was recently talking with a woman whose daughter wanted to leave her private school and attend public school with some of her friends. The mother felt her daughter wouldn't like the public school once she got there but decided to let the girl make her own choice. After explaining their concerns, the parents laid down the rules: "You can't change your mind later. If you start the school year at the public school, you'll have to finish it." The daughter insisted on going public.

A few days into the school year, the daughter was changing her tune. She hated the public school and longed for the private school she had left. But Mom, holding back an "I told you so," was sticking to her guns. The girl would have to stay at the school she hated. *You made your choice, now you have to suffer the consequences.* That's just good reality discipline, right?

Well, not exactly. The parents were about to shoot themselves in the foot. With something as important as education, you need to make the right choice, even if it means changing the rules. (Actually, I question the wisdom of giving the daughter that choice to begin with.) In any case, where "sticking to your guns" would seriously threaten the health or well-being of your child, it's best to backtrack.

6. Relationships come before rules.

The principles of reality discipline are not set in concrete. There's some give to them. People always want rules for parenting, but it's more of an art form. It's not X's and O's on a chalkboard, not arrows and straight lines. Sometimes you go with your gut, but the goal is always the same: teaching your children to love others, to put others first, to be givers and not takers, and to realize that it makes a difference how they conduct themselves.

If the discipline in your home is merely a matter of rules posted on the walls, it won't work. Oh, you may get your kids to toe the line, but they're not likely to grow into loving, responsible adults. The rules find their ultimate value as expressions of the relationships within the family. These are the expectations of how family members will love one another. As children see that their parents are committed to the family, they will commit themselves, too.

Last summer my two youngest daughters, Hannah (12) and Lauren (7), had to fly home to Arizona from Buffalo, New York. I had business back in New York, but I decided to take the flight with my girls to make sure they got home all right. Then I would just shuffle back to Buffalo on the next flight. When a flight attendant heard about my plans, she said, "You don't trust us? We offer a service where we'll take care of children on a flight and deliver them safely to a parent waiting at the gate. We can do that for you."

"That's not your job," I replied. "It's mine."

My relationship with my daughters took precedence over my business schedule, and they knew it. And I'm telling you, that's the most important bit of "discipline" I could administer in my children's life. As I signal my commitment to the relationship, they signal theirs. The same could be true for you, as you turn down a promotion at work because it would wreak havoc in your family, as you put off a business trip to see your son's school concert, as you schedule the family vacation around your daughter's soccer matches. Not that your kids are the center of the universe, but the mutual relationships within the family take precedence. If you live like that, your kids will learn to do that too.

I see many families that get their children involved in every activity imaginable. The kids carry appointment books to keep track of all their games, rehearsals, lessons, meetings, etc. As a result, the only time these parents see their kids is when they chauffeur them around town. (In fact, I have a chapter in one of my other books entitled "Help! I'm a Cabbie and My Minivan Isn't Even Yellow!" Sort of says it all, doesn't it?) But your house needs to be a home, not a hotel. You need to have relationships with your children that take priority over the slate of activities available. I love what my friend Josh McDowell says: "Rules without relationships lead to rebellion." You just can't have a hotel with a set of rules and call it a home. Life is too short not to take advantage of those formative years as your child is growing up in front of you. So don't be afraid to curtail your kids' extracurricular involvements. You need that time to build your family life.

This relationships-before-rules principle also means that you develop unique relationships with each of your children. Take time to understand who they are, with their special interests, talents, and emotional makeups. Kids are into fairness, and they'll complain if you don't provide equal treatment. They need to learn to trust you to love each one equally, even if the expressions of that love differ somewhat according to each child's uniqueness. Take the sports-lover to a ball game, the aspiring actor to a play. Give the musician guitar lessons, give the accountant a computer. Your kids may compare price tags for a while, but soon they'll get the idea that each one matters uniquely to you.

When our daughter Holly got married, the bride and groom took some time to publicly thank their parents. When it was time for Holly to thank her mother and me, she spoke only a few words, but those words said it all. "You just loved me as I was."

7. Live by your values.

Everyone's talking these days about instilling values in our children. We've got eight-year-olds watching the vulgarity of "South Park," ten-year-olds rocking to the sexual innuendo of the Spice Girls, and twelve-year-olds dolling themselves up like Britney Spears. For all too many kids today, cheating and lying are fine as long as you don't get caught—and then the response is merely a shrug and "Whatever." Society is searching for a solution.

Here's one. Live by your values.

Your children learn from watching you. What will they learn? If the cashier gives you a twenty instead of a ten, what do you do? Pocket the extra cash? Why not? Well, your kid is watching you. What will little Alphonse learn about honesty? When that driver cuts you off on the highway, what will your children be learning from you? When that attractive person of the opposite sex walks past you, when your friends start making fun of someone, when the ump makes a bad call in the Little League game—what values will your children see in you?

You can't crow about society unless you walk the talk.

Not long ago Lauren, our youngest, was carrying around a ten-dollar bill. That's a lot of money for a seven-year-old. I knew I hadn't given it to her.

"Lauren," I asked. "Where did you get that ten-dollar bill?"

She stopped short, with that cookie-jar look in her eyes, and mumbled, "Found it."

"Where did you find it?"

"In the road."

Thankfully, she's not a convincing liar. Sande was with me now, and she pressed the case. "Where did you find the money, Lauren? Tell the truth."

"In the bag."

"What bag?"

"In the kitchen."

"Now it's important to tell the truth, honey. Where did you find the money?"

And then the story fit together. We had given Kris, our married second daughter, twenty dollars to run out to the store. The bag was set on the kitchen table with the change put inside, some fifteen dollars. Whatever was in the bag had been taken out, but the money remained—until Lauren found it. Sure enough, she was now pulling a crumpled five-dollar bill out of her pocket.

How would we handle this? What measures would be in keeping with reality discipline? I suppose we could have fined her or deprived her in some way, but this "high finance" was new to Lauren. We had the feeling she wasn't quite sure what she had gotten herself into. Still, she had lessons to learn.

That night, as I tucked her in, I told a story of a boy who stole something. I was just making it up but I went the whole nine yards. The boy was arrested and thrown in jail. I wanted Lauren to know the reality of stealing.

The next day in the car, I asked Lauren, "What happens to people who steal?"

"They go to jail," she replied. Good, she got the message. But I kept revisiting it over the next few days, the stealing and the lying. She had to know that these were unacceptable behaviors in our home and in life.

Some would say Lauren never got disciplined. We never punished her for taking that money, but we taught her. We found a teachable moment and capitalized on it. In this case, words without actions seemed to be enough. If it ever happens again (and I doubt it will), you can bet that action will be swift and strong.

But that's what I mean by reality discipline as an art form. The key is to get your kids to understand the reality of the situation, to see the consequences of their behavior, and to learn to make better choices in the future. But you don't have to go overboard. I know of a man who had his two boys digging six-foot holes in the backyard for getting failing grades. His logic? They'd be digging holes the rest of their lives if they didn't do better in school. Talk about over-reacting!

I believe reality discipline is Ephesians 6:4 in action—not driving your kids up the wall as you make them ride on a yo-yo of inconsistency, permissive one minute and harsh the next. Reality discipline takes patience, skill, and a commitment to wanting to train and guide, not simply blow your cool, vent your anger, and call it "discipline."

God's love for us is *unconditional*. He loves us just because we are who we are, imperfect and prone to make mistakes. And he wants us to love our children in the same unconditional way. The desire to love as unconditionally as possible is prerequisite #1 for a parent who wants to practice reality discipline. Reality itself is conditional: If you do certain things, you face certain consequences. But unconditional love can steer us through reality's harsh lessons.

That's a crucial distinction for parents to make. You don't stop loving your kids when you discipline them. If anything, you're loving them more because you're forcing them to learn from reality. You're preparing them for a responsible life.

Prerequisite #2 of reality discipline is this: You must be willing to take the time to practice it. As I deal with parents and children, I see again and again the lack of commitment to take the time to discipline properly. We live in a society that gives us instant everything. ATM machines dot our streets, offering instant cash. People are walking around with cell phones and pagers so they never have to wait to talk to anyone. Microwave ovens put dinner on our tables in seconds rather than hours. So of course people want "instant good behavior" from our kids too.

It doesn't work like that. As someone once said, "Parenthood is a long-term investment, not a short-term loan." Parenthood involves the sting of failure and the frustration of the near miss as well as the joy of success. They all come with the territory, especially when you practice reality discipline.

Make a Difference

There are all sorts of so-called experts these days saying that we parents don't make much difference in our children's lives. They say kids are more affected by their peer group. They say biology determines the pattern of children's behavior. We give them our genes and then fade into oblivion. So goes the modern doctrine.

But let me tell you—we make a tremendous difference. If you doubt that, take a trip to the nearest penitentiary. Ask the prisoners how many come from homes where their parents loved and respected each other. See how their homes influenced their behavior.

Or go to some people you respect, people you'd like your children to emulate. Ask them how important their parents were to their current success. Sure, you'll find a few "self-made" souls who found their own way despite bad parenting, but mostly you'll find that parents show their children the path they'll follow.

Too many parents have bought the notion that they're trivial. "Experts" have intimidated these parents to the point that they're afraid to *be* parents. So they give up. They turn over their responsibilities to teachers and principals, to youth ministers and celebrities. Some of these other people are fine human beings, but they're not *you*. They're not ultimately responsible for your child's growth and well-being. You are.

Let me ask you a question. If someone knocked on your door tonight and wanted to take your car for the evening, would you give it to him? Then why would you give someone else your child? We've all been duped into thinking that activities are great for kids! *Wrong!* Kids are overexposed to activities these days, and that leads to all kinds of stress in the family.

When parents don't step up and *parent,* their kids run wild. You see them running around the mall and hanging out in front of the 7-Eleven, sneering and smoking and swearing like sailors. *Where are their parents?* you wonder. You know, those kids may be wondering the same thing. They desperately need some parenting, but their moms and dads are afraid to take the job.

I was signing books not long ago at a Walden bookstore when I saw a young boy—he seemed about six—coming toward me. He was making loud noises and flailing his arms at the books around him, knocking some off the shelves. His mother seemed tired or bored, I couldn't tell which. She said in a flat voice, "Don't touch those books. Those are someone else's." Her request didn't make a dent in his behavior.

Then the mother saw me and noticed the book I was signing—it was an earlier edition of this book, actually. Reading the title, she said, "Boy, I could use a book like that." She was right. If I'd had my wits about me I would have *given* her the book, but she was already out the door, chasing her son to the next store.

Now I don't want to diagnose this family from such a brief encounter, but it seems to me that she had given up. She wasn't being a mother to her son anymore, just a bodyguard or a cleanup crew. Maybe she'd been cowed by the "experts" who said she'd make no difference anyway. Maybe she was trying to give this youngster choices in life—choices to behave or misbehave. Maybe she didn't want to curtail his creative spirit. I don't know why she had given up, but she seriously needed to take the job of parent.

And that's what I'm asking you to do. *Take the job.* Don't leave it to the schools or the TV set. Do you really want your kid to be like all those other kids? *Be a parent.* Choose to make a difference in your child's life. Believe it or not, that's what your child wants. Every rebellious act is a plea to *Parent me! Treat me like I matter to you!*

Kids want guidelines. They need parameters. Permissiveness creates a monster that threatens *them* as well as your household harmony. When they act up, they feel bad about themselves. They need a way to set things right.

But won't it shatter their self-esteem if you correct them too much? That's another bit of nonsense pushed by those "experts." Those are the same people who don't want schools giving grades because someone might feel bad about getting a low one. And you certainly don't want anyone *failing*. I know of a school system that eliminated all F's. Now if a kid is failing, he gets a report saying he's "progressing." But how will kids ever learn if you don't let them fail?

Writing teachers now avoid correcting spelling mistakes, so they won't squelch creativity. As a result, kids can't spell. And in some soccer or tee-ball games these days they're not keeping score, because someone would lose and that might damage their self-esteem.

But where does self-esteem come from? From winning a soccer match or spelling bee? No, those victories help a kid feel good for a time, but that fades quickly. Does self-esteem come from pretending that you're doing everything right all the time? No! Lasting self-esteem comes when kids learn that they *belong*—to a family, to a community, to a group of friends. When they realize, "I can contribute, I can give something back," that's when they see how important they are. They can weather all sorts of failures as long as they know where they stand.

Too many parents are intent on giving their children everything and shielding them from every negative experience. We need to let kids become givers. Let them contribute something to the family. Let them learn what their responsibilities are. Let's set some standards for them and help them attain those standards. That's how we'll develop their self-esteem.

Don't let the "experts" raise your kids for you. Oh, you may feel inadequate, and they'll try their best to make you feel that way. But parenting isn't as complicated as the experts try to make it. It takes some effort, but it doesn't take a graduate degree. When it comes to your children, *you're* the expert. So *take this job.*

And I'm including myself in that group of outsiders who shouldn't be running your life. If you read something helpful in this book, underline it. If you disagree with something, cross it out. Feel free to modify my suggestions, if you want. If something I say doesn't quite make sense in your situation, put it aside. Use the ideas that do make sense. You know your children best. You be the judge of what works for them as you try to offer unconditional love to these special gifts from God—your children.

✔ To Review and Apply

What aspects of our modern world make it difficult for you to raise your children?

Look back over the seven principles of reality discipline. Which of those do you find hardest to understand?

✔ To Practice

Talk through the principles of reality discipline with your spouse. Decide together whether you'll put these principles into practice or not. Or do you want to read the rest of the book to see how they work?

Two

Inconsistency—
or How to Raise a Yo-Yo

Do you remember that fantastic day when your first child came into the world? I'll never forget the experience of watching my daughter's birth. What a joy it was to realize I was part of creating that miracle gift of God. My wife, Sande, joined me in celebration. All the apprehension and pain of the hours of labor evaporated when little Holly was placed in her arms—twenty and one-half inches long and as cute as they come. In the next few days I proudly showed Holly to all my friends, and I had no trouble at all coming to the conclusion that she was the most beautiful baby in the entire nursery.

We took Holly home on the third day, and for the occasion, friends put a huge sign across the front of the house that read, WELCOME HOME, HOLLY! To say I was an excited new father would be an understatement. My wife still teases me about the first night, when we placed Holly in her bassinet beside our bed. I turned up the thermostat so high it was 105 degrees in the house!

Okay, okay, so I turned the heat up a little too high. Better to be on the safe side was my motto. I was a new parent and I knew my responsibility: to take care of this totally dependent little girl.

No wonder I was puzzled when that very same week Sande's obstetrician advised us, "I want both of you to start leaving your daughter home with a baby-sitter sometime during the first few weeks of her life." I had to ask him to repeat the comment. Besides being a difficult assignment, it seemed totally inappropriate. At the very height of our newborn's dependency, our doctor was suggesting we leave her and go out for the evening.

But since then I've thanked God many times for that word of advice from the doctor. In the wisdom accumulated over many years, he knew that if Sande and I were to truly love Holly we would need to be sure to maintain a strong love between ourselves. He knew that the stronger we were as man and wife the stronger we would be as parents. So, in those very first weeks we started to develop the one essential ingredient for effective discipline in our home: love. And those first few weeks were a perfect time to begin to discipline ourselves and our new child.

And the discipline wasn't easy. It is no small trick to leave your newborn at home. Finding a baby-sitter was a major problem. There seems to be a tendency on the part of new parents to think that the only baby-sitter qualified to care for their child is a registered nurse who specializes in pediatrics or, of course—Grandma! But Sande and I took her doctor's advice and disciplined ourselves to go out at least one night a week and leave Holly home with a sitter.

I hate to think what might have happened if we had ignored our doctor's advice and centered our every move around our first-born child. She would have been like many of the children I see weekly in my private practice. These children have been brought up with the philosophy that says, "Love, love, love . . . if I just *love* little Buford enough, everything will be all right." But everything isn't all right. Children who have been given love without discipline are often disrespectful and/or too dependent on their parents.

What Nurture Is Not

Many parents often get brainwashed with the idea that nurture is built on doing everything for their children and making all decisions for them. Mothers or fathers caught in this trap might be overheard saying, "I don't care if you *are* fifteen years old, stand still! I'm going to button your shirt." If you want disaster and chaos in your life, do *everything* for your children. In the process, you will rob them of the opportunity to stand on their own two feet and to learn responsibility and accountability, two qualities that are vital in developing a well-balanced adult life.

But let's get back to our infant Holly for a moment. Was Sande's doctor telling us that we should neglect Holly, or fail to give her a lot of tender care, cuddling, holding, and so on? Of course not. All of that is absolutely critical. Psychologists call the tender loving care given by parents—particularly the mother—in the first weeks and months of life, a time of bonding. It's during this time that the parent conveys to the totally dependent infant that he or she is cared for and loved. Many studies have shown that permanent damage can be done to the personality of a newborn baby if tactile stimulating, loving, and cuddling aren't present in the first few critical days and months of life.

But what Sande's doctor was telling us was that even during infancy a parent needs to start building discipline into a child's life. By going out one night a week and leaving Holly with a baby-sitter, we began a routine that Holly soon could detect, even at her tender age. Putting a child on a schedule of one kind or another—for example, feeding, sleeping—begins to put order into the child's life. The schedule can be flexible but still teach the child order. And as the child learns order, he also learns responsibility and accountability—he learns where he fits into the entire scheme of things and what his responsibilities are.

As I give seminars on family living, parenthood, and discipline throughout the United States and Canada, I'm frequently asked questions that can be summed up in these words: "Why can't we, the parents, just make all the decisions for our kids? We know what's best for them."

I sympathize with parents who ask those questions, because I'm a parent myself. Parents do feel that they truly do know what's best for their children. And as we seek to convey love and concern to our children, we want to guide them away from some of the pitfalls of life and getting hurt. But at the same time, we should want to teach our children that they can make some mistakes. Children need to know they have the right to fail. They need opportunities to make decisions about their own lives.

Authoritarians Make All the Decisions

Many parents don't like this "freedom to fail" concept when I present it in a seminar. A few years ago, as I was speaking on the topic "Establishing the authority of God and the parent in the home," a man jumped up and interrupted, "Hey, Leman! You've gone far enough! I've heard enough of this garbage. I know what's best for my children and I'll make all decisions for them, thank you. I don't go for this giving a kid an opportunity to make decisions that can really affect his life."

I understood how that father felt, but I also knew he needed to think about what he was really saying. And so I asked him, "Who is going to make the decision for your child to accept Almighty God in his life?" The father sat down. He knew he couldn't make that decision for anyone but himself.

What I wanted that father to see is that there are some decisions we can only make for ourselves. In fact, as children grow up there should be more and more decisions they make for themselves. I believe that a critical need in homes today is that they become the kind of environment in which children can learn more about themselves. Home should be a place where children can make mistakes as they try out some things they have decided *on their own*.

Remember Ephesians 6:1–4, the passage I quoted in chapter 1? I said it would be the base for everything we would talk about. I particularly enjoy reading the first three verses. They're the kind I like to clip out, put on the refrigerator door, or pin to a child's pillowcase:

> Children, obey your parents; this is the right thing to do because God has placed them in authority over you. Honor your father and mother. This is the first of God's Ten Commandments that ends with a promise. And this is the promise: that if you honor your father and mother, yours will be a long life, full of blessing.
>
> Ephesians 6:1–3

But let's not forget the fourth verse of that passage. It has a lot to say about how we use our authority over our children, how we make decisions for them or allow them to make some themselves, and how we teach them responsibility in the home:

> And now a word to you parents. Don't keep on scolding and nagging your children, making them angry and resentful. Rather, bring them up with the loving discipline the Lord himself approves, with suggestions and godly advice.
>
> Ephesians 6:4

Authoritarianism Seems to Work

The Scripture tells us to be in authority over our children, but notice that it doesn't say to be *authoritarian*. Many of us grew up in authoritarian homes, or at least had parents who had been reared that way. Children don't have a lot of input into authoritarian systems. They just do as they're told and keep quiet. The confusing thing about authoritarianism is that it often *seems* to work. The typical pattern in an authoritarian home is a pecking order that seems to indicate that men are better than women and adults are better than children.

There was a time—between forty and sixty years ago—when our society supported the authoritarian concept. But times have changed. The problem nowadays is that children no longer view themselves as inferior to adults. They have learned to speak up and speak out and they often feel they are the equal of any adult. There is a sense, of course, in which we are all equal to one another—particularly in God's eyes. But when children feel they are the same as adults with regard to living in a household and playing a particular role in that household, the word *authority* begins to take on strange shapes and twisted meanings.

As I counsel families, I see evidence every week of how today's children are not really programmed to respond well to authoritarianism or permissiveness. In both cases, their feelings of "being equal" to Mom and Dad get in the way. Over and over, I see disciplinary problems in the homes where authoritarianism is practiced on a daily basis or where, at the other end of the continuum, children are allowed to run free by totally permissive parents.

When we deal with children from an authoritarian viewpoint, we come at them with the general attitude that we know what's best for them, we can make all their decisions for them, and they essentially don't have the wherewithal

37

to make the kinds of decisions that life requires. The authoritarian parent often backs up his "I know best" attitude with force, but that's not what the "loving discipline" of Ephesians 6:4 is talking about. Perhaps the most misused (not to mention misquoted) verse in the Bible is, "Spare the rod and spoil the child." The actual text reads: "He who spares the rod hates his son, but he who loves him is careful to discipline him" (Prov. 13:24 NIV).

The Jews believed in discipline, but when biblical writers used the word *rod* they were thinking more of correction and guidance rather than hitting and beating. For example, the shepherd used his rod not to beat his sheep but to guide them. We are all well acquainted with that phrase from the Twenty-third Psalm, "thy rod and thy staff they comfort me" (v. 4 KJV). But I doubt that many of us would feel very comforted if the Lord's rod was waling away at our heads or bottoms at every wrong turn we made.

Another thing that concerns me about the "spare the rod" philosophy is that it is based on *controlling* children rather than truly nurturing them. I've seen far too many examples of well-meaning parents who dominate their children verbally and physically. There is some strange confusion in the minds of many parents about what makes a child good or well behaved. They seem to prefer the child who is submissive, palatable, and easy to lead—sort of like a puppy.

I too want my children to be well behaved, but I'm not so sure I want them to be easily controlled by others. I want my children to be ready to move into adolescence. I want them to be ready for that turbulent world where they will be buffeted by the changing winds of peer-group pressure. I want them to be able to stand, to be responsible and mature, and to think for themselves. But if all I have done while they are young is to control and dominate them, they will be at a serious disadvantage. I prefer the concepts of reality discipline, which give my children many opportunities to make decisions, and there is no better place to learn how to make decisions than at home. I believe home should be a place where children can learn to fail and then pick themselves up and go forward.

Let me repeat that while I am critical of authoritarianism and its overuse of the "rod," I am not saying that I don't believe in taking the necessary action to discipline the child in a loving way. Sometimes—and we must be careful to know just when it really fits—spanking is the necessary action. I'll talk more about this in chapter 5. But the important thing is that the parent move quickly in every case to give the child the guidance and direction he needs to become a responsible and accountable person. If the parent fails to go into action, he winds up at the other end of the spectrum: permissiveness.

Permissiveness Reaps Rebellion

The permissive parent essentially says, "Oh, do your own thing. Whatever you want is okay." My years of counseling parents and children have shown me that in a permissive environment the kids rebel. They rebel because they feel anger and hatred toward their parents for a lack of guidelines and limit setting. Many parents might challenge me here, but I believe children want order in their lives, and even if given the opportunity to "do anything they want" they eventually come back to dead center.

In one study involving elementary grades, the children were allowed to eat anything they wanted in the cafeteria over a period of thirty days. The study showed that although the children predictably would "pig out" on sweets and other junk food first, after a few weeks they tended to go back to a quite balanced diet. I believe this study indicates the need children have for order and balance in their lives.

I'm not saying that you should give children unlimited free-dom to do whatever they want, but I am saying that in cer-tain conditions when a child does have the freedom to make choices, he learns how to make those choices in a sensible and accountable way.

One afternoon I sat in my office listening to the parents of Ryan, age eleven, who told me they were forced to lock up all their valuables (including their wallets!) in a safe-deposit box at the bank. The reason for this was simple: Ryan was robbing his parents blind. It seemed he had a heavy video-game-machine habit and also liked to indulge himself in various treats.

Ryan's behavior might have been understandable if his parents had never given him any money to manage by him-self, but that wasn't the case. Ryan had always had an allowance.

Perhaps his parents were unkind to him? No, that wasn't the problem either.

One day while I had both parents in a therapy session, the mother gave me the clue I needed. She told me rather proudly, "You know, we've never left Ryan home alone."

My response was, "That's unfortunate."

At first, the mother didn't understand what I was saying, but as we talked she got the point. By giving constant atten-tion, his parents had robbed him of the opportunity to stand on his own two feet and be responsible. And so, at eleven years old, he was behaving in a totally irresponsible man-ner and in a way that was very hurtful toward his parents.

In classic permissive style, Ryan's folks couldn't under-stand what was going on. They told me, "We've given Ryan everything he's ever asked for; we've tried to provide every-thing for him."

What a tragic misunderstanding of true parental love! Love isn't giving your kid everything he wants. If there's one thing I'm becoming convinced of, it's this: Today in our society we are raising too many children to be takers. They don't know the meaning of the word *give*, but they use another word over and over: *gimme, gimme, gimme!*

There Is a Middle Ground

We've talked quite a bit about the extremes of authoritarian and permissive parenting. We know instinctively, and through countless examples, that neither extreme works very well. What a lot of parents seem to do, however, is wander inconsistently between the two—permissive to a point, then cracking down with authoritarian wrath. I see a lot of parents in this bind. They dangle their child on a yo-yo of inconsistency, and then wonder why the kid often acts like a "yo-yo."

So, what can parents do? How do they stop the inconsistent swing between authoritarianism and permissiveness? How do they find a middle ground that makes sense to them—and to their child? There are a number of names for that middle ground, but the one I like best is *authoritative*. Don't confuse *authoritative* with *authoritarian*. There is a world of difference. Authoritative parents do not dominate their children and make all decisions for them. Instead, they use the principles of reality discipline, which are tailor-made to give children the loving correction and training of which the Lord approves (Eph. 6:4).

How does it all work? Well, suppose your seven-year-old breaks a toy belonging to another child. What should you do? What type of discipline is needed in this situation? I believe the discipline ought to be based on *reality*. The reality of this situation is that if you break someone else's property, you pay for it.

Now, you may be thinking, *Dr. Leman must be kidding. A seven-year-old kid, pay for a toy?* I'm not kidding at all. Your seven-year-old can come up with the money. It comes out of his allowance or his bank account. You'd be amazed at how many children have bank accounts before age seven. Grandmas and grandpas make a science of keeping just this kind of account afloat.

So, if your seven-year-old breaks another child's toy, you can lovingly discipline him by holding him accountable. He learns that this type of behavior costs him money.

Of course, you could give him a swat or even a hard spanking. You could scream at him, demean him, call him names, and send him to his room. All of these would be what I call punishment. Punishment centers in on the child and misses the real problem. When we punish a child, we indicate to him that we don't like him or love him. But with reality discipline, you can hold the child accountable for what he has chosen to do as you teach him the consequences of making a poor decision.

And so, in our own home, when one of our children breaks a toy, it doesn't matter whether it belongs to him or to someone else, we do not run out and buy another one to replace it. That would simply teach him or her to be irresponsible. Our children would soon get the idea they could break anything they wanted to and there would always be someone there to replace it for them. I say that is not realistic. Good discipline is always based upon the reality of the situation. And in this situation reality says, "You broke the toy; now you pay for another one out of your allowance."

In chapter 4 I will be expanding on how to use the allowance as a teaching and disciplinary tool, and it's amazing how all this works. In so many situations, you can let reality be the teacher if you only stand back and allow reality to happen.

I believe that parenting and disciplining children in an authoritative way involves at least three things:

1. *Discipline by way of action.* The discipline should be swift, direct, effective, and as closely tied to the violation of the family rule as possible. An example is what we have just

talked about. When a toy is broken, it should be replaced, paid for, or mended.

2. *Parents must listen to their children.* There is great power in listening, but few of us tap that source of power. It's just too easy not to listen—to our children, to our spouses, to just about anyone. Or, when we do try to hear what they say, we're really not listening at a feeling level and that means we're really not listening at all. I got a dramatic lesson in what it means to not be listening in a conversation I had with my own daughter. At the time I was the guest psychologist on "The Toni Tennille Show," which was then broadcast on national television. I invited Holly, our oldest daughter, to come with me to see the show.

Holly said, "Daddy, I would really like to come to the show."

I said, "Well, honey, that's why I invited you. I thought it would be a good idea to have you see how they put together a TV show, what a real television studio is like, and all that."

There were several seconds of dead silence and when I looked at Holly I saw tears in her eyes. I said, "Holly! What's wrong?"

Holly said, "Daddy, that's not what I mean."

"Well, what do you mean?" I replied.

She responded, "Daddy, after you go on TV with Toni Tennille, maybe could I just sing one song?"

Whoa! It was obvious I hadn't been listening. Holly was saying she wanted to go to the show, all right. She wanted to *be on* the show. She wanted to sing on national television! I hadn't been tuned to her wavelength at all. And once tuned in, I then faced the formidable task of helping Holly understand "reality." Gently but firmly I had to explain that I didn't have the authority to let her sing on the show, but I certainly hoped she would come along with me to watch. She finally understood!

This little incident could be passed over as just a "lack of communication." But I prefer to see it as a beautiful example of how real listening takes training. We've got to be aware of our children and how they perceive life. (We'll be looking more at this in the next chapter.)

3. *Parents should give themselves to their children.* Giving of yourself (not things) to your children is an essential ingredient for effective discipline. Many times parents apologetically ask me, "What do I have to offer my children?" I always respond, "You have yourself."

The simple truth is, children want us. They want our time. But time is very precious and most of us seem to run out of it too soon. Isn't it ironic that we often run out of enough time for our children? We somehow think that we can get together with them later. Perhaps we can start to spend more time in a few months, or possibly after the first of the year when the job settles down. Strangely enough the time never seems to magically appear. As we rush through life, time gets even more precious. And before we know it, our children are into teenage years and then grown and gone, and we never did get to know them. Instead, we tried to discipline them without really knowing who they were.

I frequently hear parents talking about "quality time." I understand what parents mean by that, but in all my years of private practice I've never heard one of my young clients (the children) mention "quality time." All a child knows is that he wants your time and your attention, whether it's to watch him do somersaults and cartwheels or to take him for a Big Mac. In trying to find time for your children, don't worry too much about how much "quality" is in it. Give them all the time you can and the quality will take care of itself. And as you give them time, you will get to know them. You will be able to build a base for action-oriented and loving discipline.

In summary, never forget that children expect adults to discipline them. If the discipline is loving, it will be geared toward instruction, teaching, guiding, and above all, holding a child accountable for his or her actions.

When a parent doesn't discipline a child, that parent invites rebellion. In essence he is giving the child a license to hold his parents in contempt. Children can actually develop hatred toward their parents if the parents don't take a stand and discipline them.

But if we take that stand, the payoff is tremendous. The following note sums it all up. It was written by that little girl you met when this chapter opened. She is that same little girl whom we started to "discipline" in the very first weeks of her life by taking one night a week to get a baby-sitter in order to keep our marriage in good repair.

When Holly was seven years old, she gave me the following note for Father's Day. The original hangs on my office wall:

Holly's spelling needs a little work, but for her dad the content more than makes up for it. Naturally, I like the "World's gatist father" line, but I am more impressed by something else. It's interesting to me that Holly used the term *discipline* rather than the word *punish*. Children *want* us to discipline them because the act of discipline shows them we care.

45

✔ To Review and Apply

What are the three types of parenting? Which has your style resembled most?

What's the difference between an authoritative style and an authoritarian style?

✔ To Practice

- *Listen.* Ask your children how they feel about themselves and their activities, school, the family, the events of the day. Really listen to what they say.
- *Spend time with your children.* Put special time in your schedule just to be with them.
- *Spend time without your children.* Get a good baby-sitter and plan a night out.

Three

It's All in the Eye of the Beholder

When thinking about reality discipline, it's always good to stop and grapple with a basic question: What is reality?

As a high school student, I was once called on to give testimony in court concerning an auto accident I had witnessed. As a seventeen-year-old, I remember thinking how odd it was that two other witnesses to the accident could be so blind. I *knew* I was right. The car at fault was the blue one, not the red one they had identified. And the blue car was headed east, not west!

In that courtroom, I learned firsthand about the concept that is often called "the eye of the beholder." Parenting your child with reality discipline has its "eye of the beholder" element also. One of your major goals in using reality discipline is to help your child think and learn. But to be successful, you have to understand what reality is—particularly for your child. No matter what you think or know about a given situation, as far as discipline is concerned, reality is how your child views that situation. What precisely happened, or what precisely is going on, is not really the issue.

It is what a child *thinks* that counts. Your child's perception of what is happening is the reality you must deal with.

In this chapter, I want to talk about three seemingly unrelated areas. All three, however, give crucial insights on how children learn and what reality is—as they see it. (For more information on birth order and its effects on personality development and marriage happiness, see my books *The New Birth Order Book* and *Sex Begins in the Kitchen,* both published by Revell.)

They Learn through Birth Order

In chapter 2 we took a look at how children perceive us when we dangle them on a yo-yo of inconsistency, somewhere between being authoritarian and permissive. The happy middle ground is the authoritative approach, which I believe is epitomized in the principles of reality discipline. When you use reality discipline, you have to be much more aware of your child's perceptions and you have to learn how to understand and relate to each child and his or her special needs.

That's why I think it's so critical to understand that the order of birth has tremendous implications for how each child in your family learns and perceives reality. Because each child operates from a different vantage point within the family, it is safe to say that each child perceives his or her family differently. For example, the first-born child has only adult models to learn from: Mom and Dad. These adult models often do things so well that it's no surprise first-born children tend to be much like "little adults."

A great deal of psychological research has been done on personality traits of children in different birth positions within the family. First borns are often achievers. They tend to walk and talk earlier and they have a larger vocabulary at a younger age. It's no surprise that later on—in high school, college, and adult life—honor societies are often glutted with first-born children.

First borns tend to be perfectionistic and will face new situations and challenges with a great deal of caution. First borns don't like making mistakes. Perhaps you can recall those times in your own life when you were in the classroom and knew the answer to the question, but for one reason or another you didn't want to speak up. This is a common trait among first-born children. First borns have a unique need to be right and "perfect" every time.

Second-born children tend to be the opposite of first borns in many ways. The second born usually has life a little bit easier than his older brother or sister, who has probably served as something of a guinea pig. Mom and Dad essentially experiment with the first-born child. The first born is brought up with stricter rules and regulations. The expectations are higher for first borns than for those who come later. That's why first borns often seem more reliable and conscientious than the siblings who come after them.

Second borns often wind up as the "middle child." Because they seem to wind up "in the middle" in just about everything, they tend to be mediators. Middle-born children like to avoid conflict as much as they can, but they are not weaklings by any sense of the term. They usually know how to fend for themselves because they have landed between two very special people in the family—the oldest and the youngest. Parents may not like to admit it but they tend to give the middle-born child less attention and therefore he learns to be more independent in all kinds of circumstances.

The child born third in the family often winds up the youngest. This youngest child tends to be outgoing, personable, and manipulative. Because she is the "baby" of the family, she is skilled at manipulating others. Just ask any first-born child. He will tell you that the baby of the family is the one who gets away with murder!

Granted, all of my observations on the tendencies of first-, second-, and third-born children are just that—descriptions of their "tendencies." There are no guarantees that children will act or develop in a certain way, no matter where they are born in the family sequence. Nonetheless, many studies bear out the validity of these general descriptions. What is important is that parents realize that each of their children has a different perception of life and reality, and much of this perception depends on where they land in the birth order. It's also important to see that with every birth or addition to the family, the entire family changes. With the birth of each child, the family unit becomes an entirely new and different entity.

The key questions for parents to keep asking as each child comes along are: "Are we making each of our children feel loved and appreciated? Are we aware of the pressures and tensions working on our family?"

There is, for example, the problem of the "dethronement" of the first born when the second child comes along. In my counseling practice with families, I see a continual syndrome: The first-born child is usually overparented. He gets too much attention. Thousands of photographs (it seems) are taken. Video documents his every move. He is definitely kingpin. Then along comes his little brother or sister and all of a sudden he seems left out in the cold. He isn't allowed to touch baby brother or sister. He can't help feed or cuddle the new arrival. And now Mommy doesn't seem to have much time for him at all because she is too busy with this new little "intruder."

Two key ways of helping your first-born child feel less intruded upon are through communication and involvement. Mom should talk to her first born while she is pregnant and explain what is happening and just what is growing inside her tummy. She can let the first born feel his little brother or sister kicking inside.

In every way she can, many months before the second child arrives, Mother can be programming her first born to be prepared for baby brother or sister and to be aware that the new arrival is going to take some of Mom's time too.

Once the second-born child arrives, the parents should do everything they can to involve the first born in its care. Even if the first born is barely two years old, Mother should let him touch and caress and help in any way possible. Just allowing the first-born child to "help hold the bottle" while feeding the new baby can be very significant.

And, when Mom gets busy with the new baby, she should continually reassure the first born that he is important too. And don't forget ways Dad can help by doing something special with the first born to make him feel extra important and loved.

As each child comes along, he or she will seek ways to identify his place in the family and ultimately in society. If each child feels loved, appreciated, and cared for, he will feel good about himself. As he goes off to preschool or kindergarten, he is much better equipped for the battle.

Parents should realize that each child's personality will chiefly be influenced by the sibling who is least like him. Take, for example, a male child who has a bright and articulate brother who is one and a half years older. Suppose older brother does very well in school (something that is not uncommon for first-born children). The second-born child may be discouraged by his brother's abilities and not do as well with his schoolwork. He may have equal ability but feel intimidated and threatened by older brother's accomplishments. So he withdraws from the academic arena, which isn't as safe or as enjoyable. The second born usually tries to find recognition in other ways. If his older brother is the scholar, he may decide to be the athlete. There are dozens of possible ways children can go. What is

51

typical is that the second born often chooses to specialize in a field where he won't have to go head-to-head in competition with an older brother or sister.

One thing is certain: Each child is unique. God creates each one with special qualities and his or her own personality. My oldest daughters, Holly and Kris, are eighteen months apart. It was always fascinating to watch them go into a store to pick out a toy or a treat. If we let her, Holly would stand there for an hour and a half and look at every possibility. She would read the directions, compare weights and sizes, and so on. Krissy, on the other hand, usually would pick out what she wanted in a few minutes or less. This is just one simple illustration about how a first born (Holly) is careful and calculating, while the second born (Krissy) tends to be more of a "free spirit."

Observe your own children and note their differences. More important, be aware of how you are responding to those differences. Are you tending to favor one child over another, in even the most subtle ways? Children are amazingly perceptive. And remember what I said as this chapter opened: Reality for your child is what he or she perceives— no more and no less. It is absolutely critical that we communicate to each one of our children, despite any differences among them, that we love and care for them *just because they are who they are.* If reality discipline is to work in your home, the ideal at which you must always aim is unconditional love for each child. That's why it's absolutely vital to discipline a child by making him accountable for his actions instead of punishing the child with verbal or physical abuse.

They Learn by Taking "Power Trips"

Every young mother knows how frustrating it can be to spend all day at home with one or more young children. It usually gets to you in one way or another. For example, it's not uncommon to hear two young mothers chatting over a cup of coffee and have one say, "Excuse me, Mary Jane, but I have to go potty." More than one young mother has confessed to me that she is ready to crack up for want of some adult conversation.

That's why I think it's crucial for young parents to find time for themselves apart from their children during the week. (Remember our doctor's advice to get a baby-sitter for Holly when she was just a few weeks old?) One of the best programs ever devised is one that I've seen started in many churches. It is usually called something like "Mother's Morning Out." Young mothers have the opportunity to bring their children to church and have them cared for while Mom goes wherever she would like for the morning. I can think of no more practical way for a church to serve a community than to allow young mothers the opportunity to get apart from their children for a few hours.

I also believe that fathers can show love for their wives in no more practical way than to help with the children whenever possible. Dad can come home from work early and allow Mom to get away to do something by herself. He can take the kids to the pediatrician and on any other number of errands. He can say, now and then, "Honey, sit down for dinner and I'll do all the serving." *That,* gentlemen, is how to really make love to your wife! As I often tell the fathers I counsel, "A man's place *is* in the home."

Getting away for even a few hours may sound great to many mothers, but some of them might wonder, *What if my child needs me?* That's just the point. Your child does not need you *all of the time.* Parents and children need minivacations from one another on a regular basis. I always tell young mothers to get all the rest they can. (They usually laugh hysterically, but I mean what I say.) Mother needs to treat herself fairly and not become a slave to her children. If Mom is always there to meet every little need the child has, the child soon becomes psychologically crippled by believing that he can exist only with Mom's presence. Another part of the "Mom is always there" syndrome is that the child learns there is a payoff in crying and fussing. The child learns that he can be very powerful, that he can use tears to manipulate Mommy and even Daddy by overly involving them in his life.

As I counsel parents and their children, I see repeated illustrations of how children learn through experimenting with power. Psychiatrist Alfred Adler calls it "purposive behavior." Adler observes that *all* social behavior has a purpose. With children, the purpose is often a maladaptive one: to keep Mom and Dad at bay, or to keep them needlessly involved in his life. To put it in today's jargon, the child takes "power trips" to see who is going to dominate, control, win, or "be the boss." And with every power trip, the child learns a little more about what works and doesn't work with Mom and Dad.

Adler points out that the very shy child can still be a powerful child. The child uses his shyness to invoke Mom and Dad's sympathy and to get them involved in his life. And by "involved" I mean overinvolved. All children are self-centered and they tend to be concerned about number one at all times. At very young ages in particular, they can't get enough of Mom or Dad and they will do everything they can to keep them dangling on a string of concern and anxiety. Show me a shy kid and I'll usually show you a very powerful little character.

Other children may use tears or temper tantrums to make their parents respond to them in certain ways. Children can actually become miniature bullies as they needlessly involve adults in their lives.

Another way to describe a child's "power trips" is to simply realize that children are always going to seek attention. They want our attention; they need adult attention; and they are going to get that attention one way or another. Ask any schoolteacher: "Do children seek attention?" He or she will always answer, "Of course they do!" And they get that attention by positive or negative means. If a child doesn't find his place at school with positive means such as making good grades, he may call attention to himself in negative ways, which cause teachers to send home notes to Mom and to make "needs improvement" notations on report cards.

Another weapon some children use to gain attention is the "I'm so discouraged" approach. Some children become quite adept at playing on Mom's sympathy as they take little power trips in the form of pity parties.

All of these behaviors are what psychologists refer to as "powerful." Powerful behavior is a child's way of saying to the parent and other adults, "I can control you. I can dominate you. I can win. I can make you do anything I want."

Powerful behavior is particularly distressing to parents. Most parents are well aware of when a child is "doing a number" on them. Feelings well up inside of us that say, "You *can't* do that to me! Don't you know who *I* am? I'm your father"—or "I'm your mother!"

Many problems between parents and their children begin right here, as the children start to experiment with power. When a child gets to that stage (anywhere from two years of age on up), he realizes he has power and he tests—with *all* his might—the limits being imposed upon him within the family. One classic form of testing is the temper tantrum. If parents can deal with these initial power plays appropriately, they will prevent a lot of problems down the line. When a child uses his temper to say, "I'm going to control you, Mom and Dad," they had better be ready to deal with the child swiftly, *and with action, not just words.*

Suppose, for example, your child has a temper tantrum while you're busy trying to prepare dinner. How do you handle it with action and not just words? Obviously you don't do a lot of pleading and imploring for the child to stop. And you certainly don't want to bribe the child with a cookie or some other reward. All of this simply reinforces his attempt to gain power and control over you.

What about spanking? Is this effective? Usually the answer is no. Spanking only increases the octaves and volume of the temper tantrum. And the child only learns that he can still control his mom or dad to some degree, even if it gains him a negative reward. In chapter 5 I'll be saying more about spanking as a legitimate disciplinary tool. Right here, however, I want to underline the fact that spanking does little good when a temper tantrum is in progress.

I believe the best approach to a temper tantrum is for the parent to pick up the child and place him in his room. Close the door behind him and let him know that he is free to have his temper tantrum in private, and that when he has calmed down, he can rejoin you or the rest of the family. It may even be necessary to remove the child from the home. Let him know that he can have his temper tantrum in the backyard and when he is finished he may come back into the house.

What do these "isolation methods" accomplish? What they say to the child is, "All right, you are having a temper tantrum, and I'm not going to stop you. But you are not going to control me by making me listen. When you can be more agreeable, we can get back together."

When you attempt to try and stop a temper tantrum with pleading, arguing, scolding, or spanking, you usually wind up with the child becoming more powerful and out of control. (Actually he is *in* control, but he seems out of control to you.) But, if you have the courage to pick up your child and place him outside the room or the house, you can be almost positive the temper tantrum will vanish immediately. Why? Because you've taken the source of power away: You have separated yourself from the scene the child is making for your benefit.

Here is the epitome of reality discipline. You are holding the child accountable for his decision to act inappropriately.

You give him the right to act inappropriately, but *not in a social situation*. You have essentially told the child, "You can behave this way if you so choose, but you are going to do it alone and you are not going to disrupt my life and the lives of others around you."

This approach seldom fails. Children are not interested in using powerful behavior without an audience. The whole point in taking a power trip is to be sure to take Mom or Dad with you. If no one is along for the ride, the power trip is just no fun at all.

"Okay," you may be saying. "That may be a good idea for coping with a temper tantrum at home in my kitchen, but what do I do when we're out shopping?"

I appreciate the problem—I really do. I've had a few like that myself. What do you do when you are in the middle of a department store, or a supermarket checkout line, and your child suddenly goes bananas? There's little three-year-old Festus, kicking, screaming, biting, and slamming his fists on the floor. What do you do? If you reach down in anger and swat Festus, the temper tantrum simply heats up. The voice goes a few octaves higher and more people begin to gather to watch you and your child in the classic power struggle.

I tell mothers and fathers who face these public temper tantrums to do something very courageous: Simply step *over* the child. (Granted, there is a great temptation to step *on* the child, but you are after positive results, not revenge.) Step over the child and walk toward the door. This sounds easy, but it could be the longest walk of your life. Take those first few steps, however, and I predict that your little one will be following you and asking you to wait. Why? Because a temper tantrum is not worth having if you don't have an audience to watch your performance.

Of course, there may be an audience of other shoppers who have started to crane their necks to watch you and Festus have at it. Hang in there and do not be manipulated. You can be sure that your child's real audience is you, not the other shoppers. He may try to embarrass you in front of the other people, but if you aren't buying, he will stop selling almost immediately. Just step over your child and walk away muttering something like, "Some people's children . . ."

And what happens if your child *does not follow you?* Walk slowly, always keeping your eye on the child. If necessary, stop near the door and do a little browsing or go over next week's shopping list. Never let him or her out of your sight, but put a good amount of distance between you so he no longer has the audience he wants: you. Eventually (before the week is out?) he will discover he's "lost"!

If the child's temper-tantrum behavior continues on other trips to the store, you may have to resort to leaving him at home. Arrange for a baby-sitter and explain to the child exactly why he is being left at home. Simply say, "Mommy's leaving you home because of how disruptive you get when we go to the store. When she has to take time out for your temper tantrums, she can't get her shopping done. When you can keep your temper better, you can go with Mommy again."

However you deal with powerful and purposive behavior, always keep in mind that every time your child takes a power trip, he or she is on another expedition of learning. He is learning about reality. If he gets away with his power plays, he learns that reality is manipulating and controlling Mom and Dad as much as possible. But if his power plays bear no fruit, he learns a different kind of reality. He learns that reality is being accountable for his actions and that unacceptable behavior has no payoff.

They Learn by Watching You

Perhaps the key way children learn as they perceive reality through their own eyes is by watching the adult role mod-

els around them. Obviously, their first role models are Mom
and Dad. As they grow older, other significant adults become
models: grandparents, brothers and sisters, aunts and uncles,
teachers, playmates, the widow next door, and many others.

Some parents may argue with me, but I still believe that
Mother and Dad always remain the key role models for their
children. I realize the power of the peer group is great. And
I realize that as children get older they often are deeply
impressed by a certain teacher, coach, or even a movie star
or professional athlete. But the ones they live with day in
and day out are their parents. Your children do learn by
watching you and, believe me, they watch much more carefully than you would ever imagine.

How then are parents to act as they go about the business
of being "role models" day by day for their children? We all
know the obvious answers: Be a good example; be consistent; your actions speak louder than your words, and so on.
I believe, however, that possibly the best way to be a good
role model for your children is to be honest.

Children, you see, start out by being totally honest. They
may learn deception and deviousness down the line, but
they start out with a very open and honest approach to life.

I recall the time I discovered a local newspaper was dropping my family advice column in favor of one on dieting
written by Richard Simmons. When my daughter Holly
heard the news, she said, "Oh, good! I *like* Richard Simmons!" Yes, children can be totally honest, even when Dad's
ego is on the line.

Sometimes a child's honesty can embarrass everyone concerned. When my son, Kevin, was nearly four years old, he
stopped one day on the way home from preschool to have
a dish of ice cream with his mother. As Sande and Kevin
were enjoying their ice cream, a woman came in and sat
down nearby. She ordered a cup of coffee and some ice
cream and then lit up a cigarette. The cigarette smoke
started to drift directly across the faces of Kevin and my wife.

Most adults who are nonsmokers are familiar with this kind of agony in a restaurant or another public place. They usually persevere in silence, but not Kevin. Kevin looked at the woman indignantly and said, "Lady, *your* smoke is getting on *my* ice cream!"

My wife cringed and blushed. The offending woman crushed out her cigarette, muttered a hasty apology, and beat an even hastier retreat.

There's little doubt that when given any kind of opportunity, children are totally honest. And yet many times I see parents trying to beat or talk that honesty out of their children. I believe this is a tragic mistake. Parents should do everything possible to nurture honesty in their children. And the best way to teach honesty is to be honest. I urge parents to be as direct and honest with their children as possible, starting when they are very young. For some reason, we don't think children can handle the truth. We tend to "cover" when we talk with them. We don't tell them everything that goes on because we feel they are "too young to understand." Although restraint is needed in some situations, I usually encourage parents to share their real feelings, problems, and concerns.

Some parents aren't sure about my advice. Won't fears and anxieties cause the child to be fearful and anxious? Well, yes, that is a possibility, if that is all you do and you are over-dramatic in the bargain. But every parent can share bits and pieces of what is really going on—the fears, anxieties, and worries. As you share your real self, your children will begin to develop an appreciation for the fact that you are not some kind of machine. They will learn that you are a real person who has feelings and needs and, yes, even failures. In short, the child will learn that you are a lot like he is. The child will say to himself, *Mommy knows what it is like to be afraid and to be worried. She understands when I am afraid and worried.*

All this may sound a bit scary to some parents who have been trained to always look as if they are in control and "competent." But I am convinced that it is important for our children to see us as imperfect. In my opinion, there is no better way to teach a child about having true faith in God. When the child learns that his parents are truly dependent upon the grace of God and that they need God's help, he will see that God is very real and not just a "belief" that is talked about in an abstract way. I always suggest that parents pray with their children as they take time to share their heartfelt thoughts and feelings. Prayer is a wonderful way to communicate with your child about the realities of life.

Being this kind of honest role model may sound a bit daring, but I believe it's well worth the risk. Here are some reasons:

1. *Through your honesty children learn that it's okay to be less than perfect.* Having faults, worries, and failures does not make a person weird or inferior. On the contrary, it is the strong person who can admit his weaknesses.

2. *As you model honesty before your child, you have tremendous opportunities to build intimacy and a strong parent-child relationship.* By being honest, you invite the child into your confidence, into your private world where few people outside the family ever have a chance to observe or listen in. In effect, you say to the child, "I trust you. I value your opinion. I know you are a capable person."

3. *As you model honesty you have opportunities to share your faith in God with your child.* You don't have to simply talk about praying to God and trusting God. You can invite your child to actually do these things with you. There is no better approach to reality than that.

Parents Need a Game Plan

Obviously, children learn in many other ways besides the three we've looked at in this chapter. But I have highlighted birth order, purposive behavior, and modeling to emphasize the importance of realizing that your children are individuals and each of them tests and discovers and learns through his own particular eyes. Reality discipline is based on understanding the uniqueness of each child, but reality discipline is no magic panacea. You don't repeat the term six times over the child and expect miraculous results every time. Reality discipline is something that must be practiced by both parents in a consistent and coordinated way. If only one parent is trying to use reality discipline, the results will be negligible. Some anonymous, wise sage has observed that you can fool an adult, but you can't fool a child. After counseling thousands of children and their parents, I agree totally. Children are so very perceptive. If they see Mom practicing one philosophy of discipline and Dad another, they will do everything they can to play one parent against the other.

I have a basic love for all children, but that love does not make me blind to reality. That's why I affectionately say, "We have met the enemy and they are small!" In many respects, children are the enemy. They act out of selfishness and concern for getting things their own way. If they see any light at all between Mom and Dad, they will find ingenious ways to drive a wedge between them. I warn parents to be on their guard or their children will make them do things or say things they will later regret.

Whenever possible, I urge a couple to do all in their power to come together and be one in their parenting. In Philippians 2:2 Paul urges all Christians to work together "with one heart and mind and purpose." Where could this advice be more needed than in the home and family! I believe it is critical that parents are in agreement while facing a child in a disciplinary situation. When parents disagree, it should be thoroughly "hashed out" behind closed doors. Talk it through and then when you come out and talk to your children and make remarks and decisions that affect their lives, they will see you working together in concert, not in disharmony.

A family lives together, but each member learns individually. Each of your children perceives reality through eyes that are unique. The child born first sees things from a much different perspective from the child born last. The child born in the middle has still another view that is especially his. Wherever they land on that birth-order ladder, you can be sure your children will be testing, probing, and using all the powers at their disposal to gain as much control as they can. And their eyes are always watching. What do they see in your home? What they see is what they will learn.

✔ To Review and Apply

How do the children in your family reflect the characteristics of first-born, middle-born, last-born, or only children? Who is most like you?

What "power trips" have you seen your kids go on?

If your children studied the way you lived yesterday, what would they learn?

✔ To Practice

- *Be honest about some fault or concern.* Make a point to tell your kids about something that's bugging you.
- *Plan your next power move.* Be ready for the next time one of your kids pulls a power trip. Write down your response.
- *Think about favoritism.* Has birth order affected the way you treat your kids? Is that fair? If something's out of whack there, make specific plans to change.

- *Tell your kids a story.* Make one up, or perhaps share a real story based on your childhood. There may be a theme in it like telling the truth, friendships, sharing, stealing, disobedience. It's a great way to slip kids a "commercial message."

Four

Why Reward and Punishment Don't Work

Most of us who grew up in traditional homes experienced the two most common methods of controlling a child's behavior: reward and punishment. Both are used on people of all ages and positions in our society. Reward has long been a standby to get others to behave the way we want them to. If we can't get their cooperation through reward, we use punishment.

Why the System Isn't Working

Some parenting theories claim that if you reward positive behavior and punish negative behavior, children are quick to catch on and soon become little angels. Many parents have tied right into this basic system of reward and punishment. But in my counseling practice, I see examples every week of why the system just isn't working. Reward and punishment may have been effective in past generations, but it doesn't take a psychologist to see that the theory is having problems as we face a new millennium.

There are several basic reasons for this. Perhaps the key reason is the strong emphasis on democracy in our present society. As soon as they are able to comprehend, children start to pick up the idea that they are equal to everyone else—including adults. From preschool through high school and college children are taught that they have been "created equal" and that they have a right to speak up. They have even decided they can "demand their rights." There have been court cases in which children have actually sued their parents for various reasons. Not only that—they won!

Obviously, there is a good side to all of this democratic teaching. God has created everyone as individuals. Certainly he loves each person equally despite size or age. Every one of us is endowed with "certain inalienable rights" by our Creator.

But the bad side crops up when children start believing they have as much authority as adults and don't need to listen to adult authority. In many school systems teachers despair because of discipline problems. And where do the discipline problems start? They start at home, where Mom and Dad have already given up and allowed little Festus to rule the roost.

For reward and punishment to be effective, the people receiving those rewards and punishments need to buy into the system. Parents and schoolteachers still use reward and punishment and will continue to do so, but the problem is the children aren't buying the way they used to. They may go along with the whole thing, but it really isn't helping them develop and grow into mature persons.

If reward and punishment no longer really work as effective disciplinary tools, what should take their place? I believe we find the answer in Ephesians 6:4, which talks about "loving discipline." The apostle Paul cautioned parents to not bring up their children in a way that would cause resentment and feelings of anger (which is exactly what reward and punishment accomplishes). Instead parents are to develop skills that focus on two other techniques. The answer to reward and punishment is loving discipline and encouragement.

Try Encouragement Instead of Reward

There is a subtle but important difference between encouragement and reward. Granted, reward works with young children. Tell the typical three-year-old you will give him a lollipop if he does what you ask and he will cooperate! Tell your twelve-year-old you will pay him five dollars for cleaning up the backyard and chances are your twelve-year-old will do the job. But sooner or later, every parent has the same question: Do I want my children to do things in the home for rewards? For example, why should my twelve-year-old clean the backyard?

1. He is a member of the household.
2. Cleaning the yard is a job that has to be done.
3. He will be paid five dollars for his trouble.
4. I want him to become involved in the family and feel a responsibility toward helping it function.

Obviously cleaning the backyard to pick up a five-dollar bill is a much different motivation from the other three. After all, it isn't just Mom and Dad's home, it's the entire family's home. They *all* live there. When it comes to doing things around the home, it's preferable that the motivation come from within, and I do not mean from within the pocketbook. If you use a reward system as the chief way to motivate your children, you are in danger of creating "carrot seekers" who are always looking for a reward (carrot) every time they do something right, good, or noteworthy in life.

To illustrate just how this works let's go back to the illustration of twelve-year-old Justin and the five-dollar "carrot" he was offered for cleaning the backyard. Justin goes out and accomplishes the task in good style and is paid his five dollars. Mom is happy because the backyard is clean and Justin is happy because he's five dollars richer. End of problem, right? Wrong! About seven days later Justin goes out, cleans up the backyard again, and asks, "Mom, where's my five dollars?"

Mom looks a bit puzzled and says, "Justin, I'm not quite sure what you're talking about. What do you mean, honey?"

"Well, Mom, last week you gave me five dollars for cleaning up the backyard and so I cleaned up the backyard again today. I'd like to have my five dollars."

You may have had a similar situation in your own home. The point is rather obvious. Once we start paying children for tasks they should be doing simply because they are part of the family, we can soon find ourselves riding a tiger. And as someone once pointed out, "He who rides a twelve-year-old tiger finds it difficult to get off."

I'm not saying that there aren't legitimate cases where you might want to arrange a special project for which your child might be paid, but the far more common syndrome that I see in my counseling work is that parents will often get suckered into having to pay their children for just about everything they do around the home. If you are slipping into this kind of trap, now is the time to put a stop to it and have a talk about being willing to develop a lifestyle that centers more on self-discipline, humility, and good works without always expecting recognition in the form of cold, hard cash.

Encouragement Emphasizes the Act

There is a subtle distinction between reward and encouragement. A lot of that subtle distinction is in the attitude of the parent and the basic guidelines the parent is laying down in the family. Let's go back to our illustration of Justin in the backyard for just another minute. In a home that was trying to stress encouragement rather than reward, how would Mom react to her twelve-year-old after he had cleaned up the backyard? First of all, she would not have dangled a carrot. She would simply have asked him to clean up the backyard because it needed to be done. Then suppose Justin did it, and did it quite well. What would Mom do and say?

I think an encouraging approach would go something like this: "Justin, what a fine job. I'll bet you're proud of yourself. That must have taken a lot of work! The yard looks really great. I appreciate your work so much. Thanks, honey."

Let's take another look at those words. Note that the emphasis is on the act and not on Justin. Mom does not say, "My, you're a good boy because you cleaned up the backyard so nicely." It's always a good idea to avoid associating a child's "goodness" with how well he does a certain task. Suppose Justin had done a rather slipshod piece of work on the backyard (a quite possible occurrence with many twelve-year-old boys). But if Justin had done a poor job, that would not make him "bad." What Mom would have to do is deal with the fact that the backyard was not acceptable. She would have to try to encourage Justin to do a better job.

In our example, however, Justin does do a fine job and Mom can tell him so. But she never links his goodness or worth as a person to what he has done. She thanks him, appreciates the work, and observes that the yard really looks great. And in this subtle way, she encourages Justin to do other jobs well, simply for the satisfaction and not for money or for some kind of label that tells him he is good and worthwhile.

What I'm trying to get at here is that we must do everything we can to encourage our children and help them see they are not loved only when they perform correctly. Love and approval based on performance is conditional. Reality discipline always seeks to love the child *unconditionally.* Our ultimate example is God himself, who loves us unconditionally with an unqualified love. We can always come to him, even when we have botched it. Perhaps the greater truth is that we can come to him *especially* when we have botched it.

In a home where encouragement and unconditional love are the real goals, the child experiences words and actions that say, "Hey, I love you—no matter what! I may not always like things you do or say, but my love for you never ends." That kind of approach is much different from the one that says, "I love you if . . ." or, "I love you when . . ." In other words, Mom will love Justin *if* he cleans up the backyard nicely. Mom will love Justin *when* he cleans up the backyard.

As Josh McDowell points out in his fine book *Givers, Takers and Other Kinds of Lovers,* loving your children if and when is not the answer. McDowell observes that the only real way to love is to simply say, "I love you." There are no ifs, or whens, or ands, or buts. You simply communicate in every way you can to your child, "I love you." Our children need to know they are loved absolutely, regardless of how they perform in different areas of their lives.

Remember that the key difference between reward and encouragement is that the reward is centered on the child himself.

"My, you're really a good boy for doing the dishes. Here's a quarter."

"My, you're a good boy for cleaning up your room. You can stay up until ten o'clock."

Statements like the above only program the child to believe he is loved *because* he does certain things. Avoid that kind of nonsense at all costs. Instead, use encouragement that zeros in on your child's behavior. As you respond positively to your child's behavior, he will feel unconditionally loved and approved.

Real Discipline Is Not Punishment

While it is difficult to distinguish between reward and encouragement, I think it is even harder to separate discipline from punishment. Like reward, punishment focuses on the child. And like encouragement, discipline focuses on the *behavior* of the child.

Ephesians 6:4 tells us to bring our children up "with the loving discipline the Lord himself approves." But just what does *loving discipline* mean? The words almost seem to contradict each other. We want to communicate love to our child, yet there are times when we have to discipline him or her. I believe the two words do go together and make sense, *if* we understand what real discipline is. I have found there are many ways to discipline a child. These methods make sense, are direct and swift, and they are action-oriented. Most important, they produce far better results than traditional punishment.

For example, Mother is on the telephone and her six-year-old starts acting up. He's loud, cranky, and is really going out of his way to make Mom's telephone conversation miserable, if not impossible. Mom chooses to ignore it and this lasts for a few minutes. Suddenly she blows her cool.

"Excuse me, Marge," she says. "I have a problem." Mom grabs her six-year-old by the neck, whacks him a few good ones, and jerks him by the arm into his room, saying, "Now, you just sit there until you can learn some manners!"

What has really happened during this rather familiar scene? Mom has tried to be patient but she lost her cool and control. She wound up lashing out to punish her child, who is now bitter, angry, and resentful. How could we rewrite the scenario to have Mom discipline her six-year-old, rather than punish him? How could we make the discipline realistic and effective?

Let's go back to the first moment the six-year-old started disturbing Mom's conversation on the telephone. It was *then* that she should have acted quickly and decisively. She could have said, "Excuse me, Marge, I have to talk to Tyler for a minute."

Then Mom could have taken six-year-old Tyler firmly, but not harshly, and led him off to another room in the house or possibly outside the house to the backyard. By doing this she would have demonstrated that Tyler could continue his behavior but he no longer had the right to do it where he was going to interrupt Mom's right to talk on the telephone. Mom could have conveyed this to him by simply saying: "I'm talking on the telephone and I don't want to be interrupted. Now you play by yourself and as soon as I'm through I'll come and tell you, and if you need anything I'll try to help you."

But notice, there would be no hitting and Mom would be in control of her emotions. And all the while Tyler would be getting discipline instead of punishment. And it would be the right kind of discipline. One thing I've learned about six-year-olds is that they don't like to be isolated. They want to hear *everything* that is going on. But for the attention-getting child who just has to keep bugging Mom or Dad while they are on the telephone, isolation is an excellent *disciplinary* measure.

Why Punishment Doesn't Work

As I have parented my own children and counseled many parents about their offspring, I have learned that discipline beats punishment every time. If punishment worked, it wouldn't be necessary to ever punish a child more than once for any infraction of the rules. If punishment really worked, the child would learn his lesson the first time around. But punishment *doesn't* work. It seems to work—for the moment—but essentially thoughts are gathering in the child's mind that run something like this: *All right, Mom, you win this round, but I'll get even. I'm gonna get you back!*

Punishment teaches children that because we—their parents—are bigger and stronger, we can push them around. We can force our will upon them. And because we—the parents—can get away with this, it reinforces the idea in our own minds that it's perfectly all right to force our will upon our children. After all, we are their parents. With some parents the problem is still more serious. We always go to our old favorite, "Children, obey your parents," to justify our heavy-handed tactics. But forcing your will upon your children isn't scriptural. We have already talked about the real meaning of the word *rod* in Scripture and how people not only misquote Scripture ("Spare the rod and spoil the child") but also misuse the entire idea of what the biblical writers meant when they talked about the rod. (See chapter 2.)

You can find no better model for discipline than Jesus himself during his ministry on earth. The Lord never beat his disciples over the head. He always dealt with them directly, fairly, and firmly. He never screamed and hollered; he never gave evasive answers. But he always gave his disciples a choice. He let them learn to be responsible and to choose for themselves. Jesus was the model teacher of reality discipline.

Granted, Jesus was dealing with adults and we are talking about disciplining children. Nonetheless, the principles are still the same. Disciplining children is difficult and it does take some skills. That's one of the basic reasons I've written this book. I want to help parents learn skills and ways of disciplining their children in all kinds of situations. I want to help parents communicate respect to children while at the same time teaching their children to respect them. Parents should always try to act in a way that enhances their child's ability to respect and honor them. Why? Because it not only builds the family but it strengthens the very fabric of society as well.

I have yet to find the Bible teaching any principle that does not build people and the societies in which they live, if they are interested at all in living correctly. The fifth commandment clearly states: "Honor your father and your mother, so that you may live long in the land . . ." (Exod. 20:12 NIV). And Paul echoed the commandment's teaching when he said, "Children, obey your parents in the Lord, for this is right. 'Honor your father and mother'—which is the first commandment with a promise—'that it may go well with you and that you may enjoy long life on the earth'" (Eph. 6:1–3 NIV).

Clearly, God's Word has set up parents with a practical and sound system. When they work the system correctly, everybody lives a longer and happier life. When the system is neglected or ignored through extremes like authoritarianism or permissiveness, things do not go well.

One of the basic reasons punishment does not work in the long run is that God did not plan for the use of punishment in a family. When God refers to his own children (believers), the emphasis is on chastisement, chastening, or discipline (see, for example, Hebrews 12:5–11 KJV, NIV). Since God created us he knows what works best with us and for us. What works best is the kind of discipline that trains and teaches in a way the Lord himself would approve.

Training Up a Child Takes Time

Proverbs 22:6 (NIV) reminds us, "Train a child in the way he should go, and when he is old he will not turn from it."

Training up a child means putting time and energy into teaching the child acceptable behavior in any number of social situations. But the bottom line is what the child does when the parents aren't there. What makes a child obey when Mom or Dad isn't around to crack down? Perhaps it's fear of punishment; perhaps it's the child's conscience.

I believe that as you train up your child with loving discipline, his conscience is developed in such a way that he is much more likely to behave properly when you aren't there. But to train him properly you must use encouragement and discipline, not reward and punishment. Parents who use reward and punishment as the two principal motivators of their children's behavior are not really helping them develop a good conscience. Instead the children learn, "I'll be good when Mom and Dad are around, but as soon as they're out of sight, I'll do what I want."

Using reality discipline in a loving way won't guarantee that your child will always be a perfect little angel, but I can guarantee that it will breed more honesty and communication between the two of you.

The best way to develop a sound conscience in your child is to teach him or her accountability. You teach accountability by setting the guidelines—the rules, if you please. The guidelines set the limits, and it's important that your children understand what the limits are and why they are there. It's up to us, the parents, to discipline our children swiftly and quietly while being open to discuss the "whys and wherefores" in a particular situation.

Another important developer of the conscience is the concept of forgiveness. We must be able to teach our children forgiveness and give them opportunities to express their remorse for violations of the family guidelines. And we must be able to express remorse ourselves. The only way we can ever teach a child to say "I'm sorry" is for him to hear it from our lips first. Parents always train up their children in the way they should go by example. Believe me, the old cliché is true: Children pay much more attention to our actions than they do to our words.

Proverbs 22:6 contains still another truth for training up children. The more correct Hebrew translation of the verse is, "Train up a child in his own way." This doesn't mean you let the child have his way and let him do whatever he wants (permissiveness). What it does mean is that every child is different. As we saw in chapter 3, every child sees the world through his own eyes. He has a certain temperament, a certain way of reacting to situations, a certain kind of personality.

When we talk about disciplining our children, we must keep in mind that each of God's creatures is created differently. No two of us are the same. I'm not naive enough to think any one method of discipline can work with every child. Because some children are more strong-willed and have a higher activity level, they will need one kind of disciplinary measure in a given situation, while another child who is more passive can be disciplined in a totally different way. Training up a child in her own way means being willing to show each child that you realize she is an individual and that each situation needs to be handled according to her needs and temperament. Reality discipline is a system that gives you the kind of latitude you need to train your children in the way that is best for them. Each child is unique. Resist the temptation to compare your son or daughter with others.

From Allowance to Accountability

Training children to be accountable and responsible not only takes time, it also takes strategy. One of the best strategies I know is in the use of the allowance to help children become accountable and responsible. Allowance is obviously not a new invention. But how the allowance is used and how it is given can make a vast difference in the behavior of your children. I suggest to the families I counsel that each child in the family get a different amount of money for his allowance (unless, of course, you have a set of twins). Age is as good a criterion as any on which to base the amount of an allowance, and it is logical that the older the child, the more his allowance should be.

I also recommend that the allowance be seen as part of the family budget. An allowance is something each child should have, just as Dad or Mom has lunch money each week. The allowance is a practical and effective way to give children the opportunity to begin to manage money, and at the same time it gives them a feeling of positive self-worth. It never hurts your self-esteem—whether you're six or sixty—to feel a jingle in your pocket that says, "Hey, I have some money of my own!"

Another obvious rule that most parents understand about the allowance is that it should come to each child on a particular day each week or month. It should be something children can look forward to on a regular basis.

I have found, however, that one thing some parents fail to understand is that an allowance is something each child should be able to spend as he or she sees fit. To give that child an allowance and then turn around and tell him how to spend it is to go right back to the problem of authoritarianism that I discussed in the previous chapters. The authoritarian makes all decisions for his child—including how the child should spend his allowance. The child learns nothing about handling money or accountability. To teach a child to be accountable and responsible, you have to create an environment in which he feels that it is safe to test and discover and learn. And he will have to learn some things the hard way. An allowance is a great tool to let him do just that.

Whenever I talk about allowances I always talk about responsibilities. Since a child is a responsible member of the household, she should get an allowance. And, because she is a responsible member of the family, she should also have certain responsibilities or chores. You can decide on these chores at family meetings at the dinner table or during other special times. The parents should be careful, however, to not make the allowance equivalent to "pay" for doing chores. The child should understand, though, that she has responsibilities. She should know that she will get her allowance simply because she is a member of the family. Nonetheless, an allowance is not completely without conditions. As a responsible member of the family, each child does have chores to help the family run more smoothly.

While I believe children should be able to spend their allowance as they see fit, the allowance can also be used as an opportunity to teach saving and stewardship. In our home, we give the child the opportunity to choose to save some of her money. When a child wants to put some of her money in the bank, I match that money dollar for dollar. We also have taught each of our children the importance of giving some of our money back to God. We try to help our children see that ideally some of their allowance should be given to God, some should be saved, and the rest can be spent as the child sees fit.

So, how does the allowance become a tool for teaching accountability and responsibility? Very simply. Suppose a child takes his allowance of one dollar (or whatever the amount might be) and blows it all on candy. And, for good measure, let's suppose that the child buys the candy while he's accompanying Mom to the supermarket. Now, remember the rule: Give some to God, save some, and spend the rest as you see fit. It will take real discipline on your part to let the child buy seventy or eighty cents worth of candy and eat it. I'm not suggesting that you would allow this to go on week after week because more is involved than spending the allowance—health and nutrition are important, too. But I believe it would be worthwhile to let the child blow his allowance for at least a few weeks in this fashion. In that way, through his own experience, he will learn that it is foolish to be extravagant and to waste his money for the entire week on candy the very first day. Invariably, during that same week, the child is going to want something else, but won't have any money, and this is where the parents have a beautiful opportunity to let reality be the teacher and disciplinarian.

There you are a few days later, in another supermarket, and your child says, "Mommy, can I have this sugarless gum?" You look the child right in the eye and say, "Brian, of course you can. Just use your allowance."

But Brian looks up sheepishly and says, "But Mom, I spent all my allowance last Monday."

"Well, honey," you say, "put it back and we'll see you on Saturday. You can buy the gum then when you get your new allowance."

The above example illustrates why I believe the allowance is such a strategic tool in teaching accountability. The allowance is a perfect way to train your children to make intelligent decisions on a daily basis. After a few negative experiences, most children learn not to spend carelessly all at once. Some of them even begin to learn to tuck away some money for the proverbial rainy day.

How to Get Those Chores Done

Don't fail to see the strategic connection between allowances and the assignment of chores or responsibilities to each child. Every child ought to have some responsibility in the home just as soon as possible. Even a three-year-old can help set the table. True, it might look like a three-year-old set it, but it is important to give each child the opportunity to take part.

Once we assign responsibilities to everyone, we face the time-honored bugaboo: What happens when the children don't meet their responsibilities, when they don't do their chores? In traditional homes, where reward and punishment flourish, Mom gets on the child's case. She yells and screams until the chore gets done. If necessary, stronger measures are used—grounding, being sent to bed without supper, and even spanking. But in a home using reality discipline, encouragement and discipline are the order of the day. When a child doesn't do his chores by the predetermined time, Mom and Dad move in swiftly and calmly to deal with the situation. As managers and leaders in the home, Mom and Dad have to decide what to do. One option is that they can hire someone else to do the job for the child. For example, if little Brian doesn't take the garbage out, perhaps his sister will. Is this imposing on little sister? Hardly. Little sister gets part of Brian's allowance for her trouble!

Notice how reality discipline works in this case. Brian loses some of his allowance, but you haven't taken it away from him to "punish" him. Essentially, he has paid money back into the family budget to have someone else take care of his responsibility. Brian may see this as punishment, so you must remain firm and gentle as you explain that punishment is not involved. There is only so much money in the family budget, and when someone else must be hired, Brian must contribute part of his allowance to get the work done. If Brian is on the ball at all, he will soon learn that losing money due to forgetfulness, sloppiness, or rebelliousness is not a very wise choice. Not only that, but he will see his money going to his brother or sister and that will *really* hurt. Chances are good to excellent that Brian will make some drastic changes in his behavior and that he will get his chores completed on time.

Hiring little sister is a perfect way to let reality be the teacher in this case. Isn't this just like the realities of everyday life? If Dad and Mom don't go to work, they don't get paid. It's as simple as that.

I am convinced that the training ground for life ought to be the home. We need to begin to hold children accountable for their decisions. In too many homes this isn't happening. Mom and Dad are always available to remind, coax, bribe, and push. Yes, maybe the chores do get done—eventually—but at what price? Part of that price is that Mom and Dad have to constantly nag the children, which Ephesians 6:4 clearly warns us not to do. But even more damaging is that through their constant nagging, coaxing, and bribing, parents are teaching their children that when they grow up and get out into life there will always be somebody there to push, motivate, and reward them for their behavior. But of course, life isn't like that. We can give our children a great tool for living by teaching them to be accountable and responsible. As the old saying puts it, teach them to stand on their own two feet.

Variety Is the Spice of Responsibility

Before leaving the topic of chores and responsibilities, we should take a good look at the concept of variety. The bad news about chores is that they have to be done; the good news is that they can change. Buford doesn't have to look forward to being the "garbage man" for life. The job can be passed down to a younger brother or sister as he grows older.

In fact, I surprise a lot of parents with my recommendation to give their older children *less* to do. My reasoning is this: I believe that as a child grows older and gets into high school he faces much more pressure by way of academic challenges and extracurricular activities. I believe the high schooler's chores in the home should decrease and that the younger children in the family should take up the slack. For many families I know, the reverse seems to be true. The older children are saddled with responsibilities and they continue to be responsible year in and year out while their younger siblings get off with less to do.

If you have children from teens down to younger years, think about it for a moment. What responsibilities did your sixteen-year-old son have when he was ten? Compare those responsibilities with your ten-year-old daughter's responsibilities today. In many families I counsel I find that the sixteen-year-old had more responsibilities when he was ten than does his ten-year-old sister today.

The challenge for parents is to keep moving responsibilities downward in the family and to be ever aware that the younger children should have the opportunity to pitch in on an equal basis.

In fact, as I said, if at all possible teenagers should be given fewer chores to free them for studies, extracurricular activities, athletics, and all the other pressures that come their way in high school. I'm not saying that teenagers should be allowed to sit back and do nothing while their younger brothers and sisters are doing all the work around the house. And it may not be possible to relieve teenagers of certain chores. Perhaps they don't have a younger brother or sister who could step in at that particular point, or there may be some other problem. The rule of thumb that I urge parents to seek, however, is to spread the responsibilities around and try to relieve the teenagers in the family of as much pressure as possible while helping the younger children learn accountability and responsibility at their end.

Naturally, once the teenager is relieved of some of the chores and responsibilities, he then has to be accountable for how he uses his time. Goofing off, not studying, and just hanging around and getting into trouble are all unacceptable ways to use free time. Talk with your teenager about his responsibilities. Explain that you have tried to lighten the load at home so that he can meet the heavier responsibilities at school.

It's Never Too Late to Start

On the other hand, you may be wondering why I am making so much out of assigning responsibilities and chores. In many homes today, in suburban America in particular, finding chores for children is almost a lost art. Many adults can remember how they grew up in rural settings where they experienced definite responsibilities. Chores they had to do made a noticeable impact on the well-being and even the income of a family. Today, however, we have moved in the other direction, toward being sophisticated and soft. It's easier to hire a gardener than hassle Jason about mowing the lawn. In the interest of time or convenience, we fail to provide our children with opportunities to become accountable and responsible in the home by meeting certain definite responsibilities daily or weekly. I believe that a major challenge for parents today is to always be seeking ways to divide responsibility among family members in a fair way. The responsibilities may vary and they can change from time to time (for example, when children become teenagers), but everyone should have something for which he is accountable.

If you believe you may fall into the category of parents who haven't done as much as they could to give their children opportunities to be accountable through family responsibilities and chores, it's never too late to start. But I suggest you start in a low-key manner. Sit down and talk with your children and allow them to pick and choose what their responsibilities might be. List all the jobs that need to be

83

done. The entire family could help identify what all these jobs are. Write all the jobs down and then assign various tasks. Try to allow the children to choose their tasks, but if there is squabbling or bickering, you may just have to arbitrarily assign certain duties with the comment, "Let's try it this way and see how it works." Keep reminding your children that being assigned a chore is not a life sentence. Keep the entire situation flexible. Remember that what you are really after with the assignment of responsibilities is to teach your children to be accountable and responsible.

I have talked a lot about accountability and responsibility in this chapter. We have looked at the difference between encouragement and reward as well as the difference between punishment and discipline. Perhaps we need to look further at just how reality discipline works when children don't come through. What happens when they don't cooperate? I have a favorite little saying that I use in my seminars and counseling sessions: "Sometimes you have to pull the rug out and let the little buzzards tumble."

Parents usually chuckle as they picture their "little buzzards" tumbling about. Of course, I caution them that whenever you "pull the rug out" on a child you do it in a way that teaches him and doesn't hurt him. In the next chapter, we'll take a detailed look at just how to pull the rug.

✔ To Review and Apply

How does reality discipline differ from a reward/punishment system?

How can you encourage or correct your children without defining them as "good" or "bad"? Why is that important?

✔ To Practice

- *Rehearse your encouraging words.* What will you say instead of "good girl" or "bad boy"? Practice wording that supports without defining. "Good job—now you're getting it."
- *Divide your labor.* If you haven't done so, divide up family responsibilities, assigning appropriate chores to different children. Discuss appropriate allowances.

Five

"Pull the Rug Out and Let the Little Buzzards Tumble"

"Actions speak louder than words."

This has become a cliché, but it remains as true as ever, especially in regard to child rearing. Our kids do pay attention to what we do, and they don't always pay attention to what we say. That's why I say, "Sometimes you have to pull the rug out and let the little buzzards tumble."

If you're a mom, you may shudder a bit at my referring to your gift from God as a "little buzzard." And perhaps "pulling the rug out" sounds more like punishment (maybe mayhem) than discipline. Please bear with me. I'm from Tucson and here in Arizona we like to think "little buzzards" are cute—especially the ones who roost on our backyard swing sets. As for "pulling the rug out" being punishment and mayhem, not so. To pull out the rug is the key to making reality discipline work. Let me show you why.

A couple of years ago I worked in counseling with Eric, age ten. He lived in a rural community and liked animals a great deal. Without his parents' permission, he bought (with his own money) two baby pigs from another boy. Eric brought his pigs home and showed them to Mom. Mom wasn't ready for baby pigs and told him he would have to get rid of the little porkers; they simply couldn't stay. Two weeks later, however, the pigs were still there. Eric had used all the tricks on his parents: He had already spent his money; he couldn't take them back; he would take good care of them and raise them up, sell them, and even make some money, and so on.

But Eric's mother simply couldn't agree to having those pigs around. Eric stubbornly insisted on being granted the privilege of keeping his pigs. The whole thing was turning into something of a family pork-barrel scandal when the parents sought me out as counsel.

My recommendation was swift and brief: Get rid of the pigs. Their response beautifully illustrates the dilemma parents find themselves in when they're not willing to pull the rug out. How could they get rid of the pigs when they belonged to Eric, they wanted to know. And where could they take them?

I challenged Eric's parents with the thought that their child had been irresponsible when he brought home two animals to the family farm without the consent of his parents. I reminded them that as Eric's parents they were in authority over him. When a child steps over the line and by his actions says, "You're not my authority—I'll do my own thing," parents have the responsibility to act quickly and decisively—and pull the rug out.

Eric's parents got the message and got rid of the pigs. In fact, they got rid of them rather easily by finding another family who was willing to take them—without having to pay for them. Of course, Eric wasn't very happy. He lost all the money it cost him to buy the two pigs. And that just might have been the best discipline in the whole affair. It was a consequence his parents had to let happen.

When Eric came home and discovered his pigs were gone, he was outraged. In fact, he was beside himself. But his parents told me later that this "rug-pulling" incident with the pigs really got Eric's attention. It led to some positive changes in his behavior.

As I'm sure you have already suspected, the pig incident wasn't an isolated case in Eric's life. He had already been trying to prove he could "do his own thing" in many different ways. Still, it wasn't easy for Eric's parents to see him lose the money he had worked so hard to earn by doing chores on another farm. Nonetheless, it was a great lesson and he learned it the hard way. Mom and Dad had been very patient during the two weeks they had reminded and coaxed him to get rid of the pigs. There was a good possibility he could have taken them back to the farm where he had bought them. His friend may even have given the money back. But Eric was so determined to do his own thing that he didn't bother to try, and he paid the price.

As distasteful as pulling the rug out from under Eric was, it was still the best discipline (and love) his parents could possibly demonstrate. My counseling and speaking in seminars across the country has convinced me that parents have been sold a bill of goods. They have heard that psychologists believe a child's psyche is so fragile that we shouldn't hurt or upset the child in any way. I agree with Ephesians 6:4. We shouldn't frustrate our kids or "provoke them to wrath" (see KJV). But to say they are too delicate to learn from discipline based on love and reality is foolish.

As I mentioned in an earlier chapter, children will constantly test their parents. They don't test us out of pure orneriness; what they really want to know is whether or not we care. When we are firm and prove that we do care, they may not like it but they do respect us and appreciate us. Let me repeat that "firm" discipline is not punishment. In this particular situation with Eric and his pigs, the loss of his money (not to mention the loss of the pigs) provided a perfect form of discipline. What would have been inappropriate—and probably of little effect—would have been screaming, name-calling, or spanking. And right here is as good a point as any to talk about that most traditional form of "discipline" of them all: corporal punishment. You may have been wondering whether I believed in it or not. Read on.

Does Pulling the Rug Out Ever Include the Paddle?

Yes, I believe that spanking does fit into my rug-pulling philosophy. But spanking has to be used in the appropriate situation. For example, a swat on the bottom can be a good disciplinary measure for a young child in the two- to seven-year-old range when he is being absolutely willful and rebellious.

Go easy, however, on swatting children under two years of age. I believe children eighteen months and younger should never be swatted. A child that young doesn't understand what is happening. In fact, children under eighteen months do not have complete conceptual development. *No* is not a word they really understand. (Yes, I know they seem to, but what they are understanding far better is the look on your face.) When you say "Come here" to an eighteen-month-old, it is usually an effective way to get him to run in the other direction. Children at this stage are "oppositional." That is, they often want to do the opposite of what you suggest. Holding out a toy or the child's "blankie" is a much more appropriate means to get the child to come to you.

As children reach the age of two, they are more capable of conceptualizing. They are also getting past the oppositional stage. Many mothers would disagree with me there because everyone is familiar with the "terrible twos" syndrome. Nonetheless, at two and above, most children can understand a request such as "Come here" but they may be defiant and refuse to come. We are all familiar with those

89

times when children do force us into a showdown. In situations where it's a case of Dad or Mom winning or Festus winning, my money is on Dad and Mom every time. If a swat is necessary, so be it. The reality that I've seen in family after family is that if little Festus wins, the game is over and discipline is down the drain.

The Right and Wrong Way to Spank

There is, however, the right and wrong way to spank. Entire books have been written on the subject, but here are some guidelines.

The key to spanking a child is being in control of your own emotions. While it seems a contradiction, spanking is something that must be done in love. True, you may not feel very "loving" while administering the spanking, but the way you show your love is by not losing your cool.

There is a world of difference between one or several good swats and beating on a child in absolute rage, which is usually accompanied by shouting and verbal abuse.

The second key principle to apply when spanking is what I call "follow-up time." Some writers on discipline and child rearing indicate that once the spanking has been administered, a child feels that he has paid his debt and therefore the situation has resolved itself and is over. I'm not comfortable with leaving it at that. I believe that when you spank a child, you have an obligation to tell the child exactly why he was spanked. You have the further obligation to listen to the child. Immediately after the spanking may be a good time for him to talk about his feelings: what made him angry, what made him say what he said or do what he did, and so on. The parent, as well as the child, can always learn from these situations. And it's even possible that the parent will learn that he acted in haste and perhaps spanked for the wrong reason. If that happens, the parent owes the child an apology and it should come immediately.

The key to follow-up, however, is physical contact. Hold the child and talk to him about your feelings. Explain why you were upset. Explain what made you angry and why it was necessary to spank. And explain what you expect from the child in the future.

It's quite possible the child may want to apologize or show remorse. He may say something like, "I'm sorry, Mommy." If he does, encourage him in a warm and loving manner. You may wish to say that you are sorry too but you had a responsibility to spank in order to teach him the right way.

Always try to reassure your child, particularly if he is between the ages of two and seven. During the "follow-up time," tell him you love him. Explain that there will be times when he will do things that are wrong, but even though he does these things you will never stop loving him and caring about him.

So much for some general rules for spanking. But a lot of parents want to know *when* they should spank and *why*. I believe that spanking is particularly helpful with young children when their safety is involved. For example, a two-and-a-half-year-old may repeatedly get too close to a swimming pool or some other dangerous area. If he willfully disobeys a mother's instructions, it can be very effective to give him a swat and move him to safer ground. If he repeats his violation, you may need to give him another swat and isolate him from the pool area by keeping him in the house.

The same principles hold true for children who constantly run toward the street and fail to obey Mother's admonitions to be careful. Some child-rearing specialists advise never to swat a child with your hand. They say to use a ruler or a paddle. I disagree with that approach. I believe that love and discipline go hand in hand (pun intended). Proverbs 13:24 says if you love your child you will discipline him. The same hand that guides a child across a busy street must sometimes discipline to help him learn. The key to spanking is to do it with love.

Be Sure They Feel Loved

Like any form of discipline, spanking is more effective when the child feels loved. I like the advice by Larry Tomczak in his book *God, the Rod, and Your Child's Bod.* I must confess, the title threw me at first, but Larry's approach to spanking as "the art of loving correction" is sound. Tomczak gives some practical suggestions for making a child feel loved. They include:

1. *Make sure you see your children as God sees them*—as a "gift," a "reward," and as "arrows" (Ps. 127:4)—not as an interruption, accident, or tax break.
2. *Cultivate a childlike attitude.* Don't take yourself too seriously. Rediscover play. Walk barefoot together across the wet grass. Ride a merry-go-round. Act out a story instead of merely reading it.
3. *Give your children direct eye contact.* A child has a critical need for focused attention that enables him to feel respected, important, and loved. "Daddy (or Mommy) really cares about me . . . what I say . . . what I do."
4. *Physically express your love.* Regular hugging, kissing, sitting close together, tousling hair, tickling, rubbing backs . . . putting an arm on the shoulder . . . are all absolutely essential to assure a child's emotional security and to nurture his self-esteem. They communicate this thought: "I like you and enjoy being with you." These are the building blocks of a strong, healthy love bond.
5. *Train yourself to be a good listener.* Listening requires discipline, especially with children who can tell you the

same Winnie the Pooh story a hundred times. It involves the eyes, ears, mind, and heart. It means kneeling at times so as to be on their level and to communicate eye to eye. It's important that as parents we respond to our child's feelings. Such statements as "Not now, I'm busy" or "Tell me later" say to a child: *I guess I'm not as important to Mommy and Daddy as other things are.*

6. *Spend . . . time together.* There simply is no substitute for regular, consistent time spent together doing ordinary things (eating, working, walking, praying, driving, swimming, shopping) or "making memories" by doing extraordinary things (visits to a zoo, pet shop, amusement park, or hospital; playing table games, attending a sandlot softball game; picnicking, camping, biking, hiking, building a model plane; sewing a doll's outfit; sight-seeing, visiting museums, visiting your nearby fire station, and taking them for a tour of where Dad works).

I especially like what Larry Tomczak says about listening and spending time. Spending time with your children does create great memories. A child's life is so pliable during the formative years. Do your best to give your child a great gift every day: *yourself!* And be sure to listen. All parents look back and realize how quickly time passes. Use your time wisely. Listen to your children when they are little. They are much more likely to talk to you when they are older!

Respect Is a Two-Way Street

Spanking is a possible option for disciplining your child, but always be sure you are doing it as loving correction, not in any way that rejects your child. As Larry Tomczak says, if you find it necessary to administer a swat, do it not to humiliate or embarrass or to be cruel and harsh.

While spanking is an option for discipline, I believe it seldom should be the first choice when deciding on the best way to "pull the rug out" to help your child learn. I think life's best teachers are experiences in reality. I'm not saying spanking isn't reality, but I am saying that reality includes so many other approaches to loving discipline.

For example, you can use the power of choice—that is, you can give your children choices. Many hassles develop in families between parents and children because of power struggles. In any parent-child relationship, there are bound to be times when there is a conflict of wills. Mother says Megan will wear a certain dress and Megan says she won't. Mother says she will and Megan firmly resists again. And the war is on.

How can this kind of struggle be avoided? How can Mom teach her daughter to respect parental wishes? The obvious answer is for Mom to try to show her daughter some respect as well. And how can Mom accomplish this without giving up all of her authority? One possibility is to separate the clothes in Megan's closet—clothes for play and school on one side and clothes for Sunday school, church, and special occasions on the other. Then Megan can make a choice and feel that she has some control over her own life.

You can go still further with the clothes closet arrangement and possibly break the clothes for school into certain categories; and you may want to put clothes for play in still another section.

As you make changes in a child's wardrobe, depending on the season, you can glean out clothes that no longer fit or that are inappropriate for one reason or another. You may want to involve your child in the gleaning-out process.

Through all of these simple actions, you will be allowing your child to make more and more decisions for herself. To be able to make some decisions for herself builds self-esteem and confidence. The child feels respected and will in turn be more likely to respect the parent. When a parent gives a certain amount of freedom to a child regarding choice of what the child might wear, the child often comes out dressed and asks for Mom's or Dad's approval concerning what he or she has on. This is just one simple example of a basic principle: If we do our job as parents and use our authority wisely, our children will respect us and our opinions.

Don't Demand Respect—Earn It

Granted, however, you don't gain your child's respect by using one simple strategy such as giving choices concerning what to wear. Like most important things in life, respect is not something you obtain easily. And another thing that parents need to realize is that they can't *demand* respect from their children. Oh, I suppose you can demand it and all the while be pointing at Ephesians chapter 6, which clearly states that children are to respect their parents. But that may not cut much ice with little Snookie or Cletus. The way to gain respect from another person (and it helps to remember that our children *are* persons) is to earn that respect. You can't cook up respect in a microwave—it takes time to develop.

I remember going to the hospital to visit a fifteen-year-old girl who had tried to commit suicide. Her family contacted me immediately and asked me to pay her a visit. I cleared my schedule and went right to the hospital. As I was walking up to her room, questions flooded my mind: Why would this girl want to take her life? What kind of predicaments and problems did she face?

When I got to her room I found a beautiful teenager who was completely distraught, in tears and total depression. I asked her if she knew who I was and she said, "Yes."

I sat next to her, beside her bed, and simply asked, "Do you want to talk about it?"

She didn't answer. Instead she stared at the ceiling, and the look on her face said quite plainly: "No, I *don't* want to talk about it."

I sensed that she was testing me to see whether I really cared about her or whether I had been sent by her parents as some kind of stooge or spy.

"If you don't want to talk about it, we don't have to," I said. "In fact, you don't even have to see me or put up with my sitting here, but I do care about you and your family and if there's anything I can do to help, I want to do it."

I went on talking and shared a little of my own life with her. I shared some of my intimate thoughts and feelings about teenagers I had worked with and the problems I had seen in families. As I talked she stopped crying and began looking right at me. I almost cheered out loud because I knew that eye-to-eye contact with this desperate girl was a special breakthrough. As we talked and I continued to show her I wouldn't condemn her, she began to open up. And of course, when she began sharing what was inside, out came a lot of hostility and anger. As we talked, the hostility and anger seemed to lessen slightly, and I finally asked her if it would be all right to come back and see her the next day.

"That will be okay," she said, and we exchanged waves as I went out the door.

I was back the next day and she looked a little better. She seemed to be in better spirits but still depressed. As we wound up our second conversation, I made a specific point of telling her that she didn't have to talk to me or see me anymore. It was something she'd have to decide. I only wanted to be there if I could really help her.

It was then she asked me the question: "Well, what do you think I ought to do about my problem?"

At that moment I knew I had finally broken all the way through. Now she was asking my opinion. By asking that question she was saying, "I value your opinion; tell me what you think."

I had finally earned the girl's respect. I had paid my dues and she was now interested in knowing what I thought about what she should do. This is what respect is all about.

It would have been easy to walk in and be very "professional" with the girl. It would have been easy to put her on an even deeper guilt trip than she was already experiencing. Instead, I had to be soft, gentle, and understanding. I had to show her I cared, and I did care!

The ending of the story is a positive one. The young lady got her head straight, overcame some of the overwhelming obstacles she was facing, and made good progress in a relatively short period of time.

In some ways, of course, it might have been easier for me to earn the respect of the desperate teenager in the hospital than it is for a parent to earn the respect of little Festus or Zelda on a 24-hour-a-day, 365-days-a-year basis. But it can and must be done. And one of the telltale signs that you have your child's respect is the question, "Hey, Mom [or Dad], what do you think about this?"

Naturally, you won't always agree with your child on everything. But as long as you have love and respect for each other, the relationship will grow and become stronger and stronger. I often tell parents of younger children that now is the time to build respect between you and your child. It will be like money in the bank when your child hits the teenage years and tensions mount.

From Giving Choices to Pulling Rugs

But what, you may ask, does building respect and giving choices have to do with "pulling the rug"? A great deal, as the following illustration shows.

Choices have to be appropriate, of course. You don't talk with a twelve-year-old about whether or not he wants to drive the family car. You don't tell a six-year-old that he has a choice: He can play with his toy truck or Daddy's shotgun. But many everyday choices are there for the child to make, if we allow him to do so. We can give him the choice of what he wants for lunch that day: "Matthew, would you like a tuna sandwich or peanut butter and jelly?"

We give Matthew the choice, but we teach him that once he makes his decision he does not have the prerogative to change his mind. If we want to use reality discipline, we have to show Matthew that if he changes his mind there will be a consequence of some kind. That's how life works. In other words, we must hold him accountable for his choice.

But what happens in many homes? A typical scene is that after Matthew chooses peanut butter and jelly and Mom has it all prepared, he decides he wants tuna instead. So Mom wraps up the peanut butter and jelly and tries to save it for another day and dutifully makes Matthew his tuna sandwich.

What is Mom teaching Matthew when she allows him to change his mind at this point? Ironically, she is teaching Matthew to be irresponsible because she is taking an irresponsible position. Here is a beautiful opportunity to let reality come into Matthew's life and teach him a truth that he can use all his days. What I am saying is this: Give Matthew the choice between eating his first choice (peanut butter and jelly) or not eating at all. If Matthew chooses not to eat peanut butter and jelly, don't force it down his throat. Put it away and try to keep it fresh for later. But for Matthew, lunch is now over. He is free to play or do whatever he wants to do, but he gets nothing else to eat.

Matthew may shrug and go off to play, but reality may soon move in to teach its lesson. Reality will come in the form of hunger.

Before dinner—quite possibly *well* before dinner—Matthew will be back to the kitchen whining about how hungry he is. This is a crucial moment for at least two reasons:

(1) Mom may feel a pang of guilt and sympathy for Matthew, but she must pray for strength and not give in. (2) She must explain to Matthew why he can't have anything to eat until dinnertime. She has to tell Matthew clearly and simply that making decisions is important—even simple ones such as what sandwich we plan to eat. She might say something like this: "Yes, I'll bet you are hungry. Since you didn't eat any lunch, you must be starved! Well, you're in luck. We're going to have dinner in about two hours and twenty minutes, right after Daddy gets home. Now run along and play and we'll see you at half-past six."

And so, clutching his hunger-knotted stomach in agony, Matthew goes back out to play. He may shed a tear or two, or at least make some remarks about how mean Mom is. But reality has now moved in to finish "pulling the rug." The rug pulling started back at lunch when Mom put away the peanut butter and jelly sandwich, but refused to make the tuna. Now that Matthew faces a little real hunger for a couple of hours, the rug has been pulled indeed.

And what has Matthew learned? The goal is to teach him that it is a poor decision not to eat what Mom prepared for lunch. It is a poor decision to change your mind after it is too late. It is a good decision to go ahead with your choice, even if you believe you might prefer something else at the moment.

Taking the Buzzard by the Beak

Does all this sound too mean and heartless? Some mothers I counsel accuse me of having a cold, "male-oriented" attitude.

"It's all right for you, the father, to talk about letting the child go hungry," they say. "You're at work and you don't have to look him in the eye."

I tell these mothers that I understand. At our house, Sande and I try to split up the rug-pulling chores as much as possible. As for being "cold," I smile and say that nothing could be further from the truth. For proof I invite the protesting mother to ask my own kids if I am cold and cruel. Sande and I have been pulling the rug and letting our little buzzards tumble all their lives, and they don't appear to be any worse for the wear. The reason? We love them with all that is in us and they know it!

We don't pull the rug out as a form of punishment or vengeance. We don't pull the rug out to dominate our children or take parental ego trips. We pull the rug with love (and sometimes it takes tremendous commitment to do it because it hurts). It would be easier to just hug them, cuddle them, and coddle them, but this would not teach them the accountability and responsibility they need to face life later. There will be a day when your kids are too big for a lot of hugging and cuddling. And that is when your love can still touch their lives in a tangible sense as they go about the task of being accountable and responsible adults.

I also like to think that pulling the rug out is a good way to emulate the master role model of reality discipline—our Lord. Yes, he taught us to turn the other cheek, but on many occasions he took the bull by the horns and got things done. He was kind and compassionate, but he was also firm and direct as he pulled the rug on Peter, James, John, the rich young ruler, and many others.

And that's what reality discipline is all about: going into action, taking the bull by the horns (more precisely, taking our little buzzards by the beaks), and pulling the rug with kindness and compassion. There is no better way to demonstrate real love.

I recall one family in which the parents were ruled by Todd, age five. Pulling the rug was a totally repulsive idea for Todd's parents—especially Mom.

Todd was the baby of the family and like many children born last, he was fussy. He liked only certain things, especially when it came to eating. He liked potatoes mashed, but not boiled or baked. He liked his pancakes spread out on the plate not stacked on top of one another. Todd was indeed a picky child and somewhat of a perfectionist.

Naturally, there were all kinds of hassles at meals. Todd's older brother and sister would usually eat whatever was put before them, but not Todd. He often turned the family dinner hour into a mini war.

Todd's father did not share his son's perfectionist approach to pancakes or potatoes. He had been raised to not speak unless spoken to and to do what he was told and that was it. Having a child who would rebel over something as simple as eating or not eating his dinner was too much for Dad to take. Down would come his fist on the table and terror reigned supreme. But it seldom got Todd to eat any better.

I tried to help these parents by telling them that they need to give children choices. I explained that the family dinner table is a perfect place to give a child a choice to eat or not to eat. I helped them outline a simple strategy and they went back home to put it into action.

Dinner that evening featured fried chicken. Todd took one look and one sniff and said, "I don't like it! I don't like chicken."

Mom was puzzled because Todd had eaten two helpings of chicken last week, but she didn't go into her usual routine of, "Honey, of course you like chicken. Just last week you had two helpings, and besides, if you eat your chicken you'll get your special strawberry shortcake for dessert."

I had explained to Mom that this kind of talk is useless and even harmful. It doesn't do a thing to get a child to eat.

Instead, Mom quietly picked up Todd's plate, went over to the kitchen sink, and with a flick of the wrist, Todd's dinner was over.

Now, I'm not sure what went through Todd's mind but he might have been thinking, *Mom has finally flipped. She said I was driving her crazy and I think it just happened. She's always telling me how much food costs and she just threw my dinner in the garbage.*

Was Mom's action too severe? Should she have talked it over with Todd and tried to reason with him? She had already tried that many times. No, I believe her action was correct. It is always the perfect disciplinary action with kids who won't eat what is put before them. It actually gives them the right to choose either to eat or not to eat. And it holds them accountable if they choose to be picky or fussy, because the final pull on the rug in this case is that there are no snacks, no treats, nothing at bedtime. They are free to leave the table. They can play, do their homework, whatever their usual routine is, and there will be no punishment. But there is discipline. And the discipline says, "Hey, Mom and Dad aren't going to play the bribery game. We aren't going to have a hassle and shouting and slamming fists on the table. We're just not going to play that kind of game anymore. If you don't want to eat dinner, dinner is over. There will be no cookies, no treats, no anything. It's just good-bye and see you at breakfast."

In Todd's case, his mother recalls that he ate one of the biggest breakfasts of his life. And after that first heroic move on her part (and I use the word *heroic* because I know how hard this was for Mom), she started giving Todd other choices but never the choice to be picky or fussy. And life improved immeasurably in that family.

When parents are brave enough to pull the rug out, they are giving their child the best training possible. They are giving him the opportunity to make a good or poor choice. I believe home should be the place to make good or poor choices. The last place home should be is a place where you are punished for making poor choices. In too many homes I see parents making far too much out of too little. When the milk spills, or the spaghetti is dumped on the dinner table, we don't need sharp words, shouting, a slap, or a thrashing. We need a rag and a kind word that lets the child know that "accidents happen."

Of course, kids don't always think that pulling the rug and using the principle of action and not words is fair. As I said in an earlier chapter, they are masters at trying to put parents on guilt trips. They argue with the skill of accomplished lawyers about what is fair and not fair, when they've been warned and haven't been warned.

But parents have to be firm. They should set up the guidelines and let the child know that if he crosses the line, the rug will be pulled.

For example, parents often complain that their children abuse their toys. I tell them that if little Brandon seems to be doing his best to disassemble his video game, simply move in and calmly take the game away. Yes, little Brandon may be upset, but you will accomplish several things. You save the toy and demonstrate to Brandon that toys cost money and we don't abuse them. More important, however, you keep order in your home and teach Brandon to have respect for his possessions as well as yours.

Taking a toy away from a young child who is playing with it in a destructive manner is not punishment. It doesn't say, "I don't love you." It doesn't say, "I don't care about you." What it does say is, "As your parent I can't allow you to misuse this toy. Toys cost money and you can't destroy them just because you think it's fun."

What about a situation where the child actually breaks a toy (or anything else for that matter)? If the child is old enough to get an allowance, an excellent disciplinary measure is to have him pay for a new toy out of his own money. Here is another example of how the allowance can be a tremendous teacher of accountability and responsibility. It's interesting to me that the picture most people get when I talk about pulling the rug out is that the child will land right on his wallet. And, of course, when I talk about pulling the rug, I'm not talking about actually trying to hurt the child in any way. But when you can have the child learn through realizing that poor decisions and poor behavior result in paying through the pocketbook, you are giving him a taste of reality indeed.

Anything Is Easier Than Real Discipline

Basically, I have used this entire chapter to demonstrate one thing—anything is easier than real discipline. It's much easier to be permissive and to just "let it go." And it is even easier to punish because you allow yourself the luxury of letting off steam and you usually don't have to follow through and make sure your child actually learns something. We like to think we'll "teach little Brandon a lesson" by spanking him, berating him, and sending him to his room. Unfortunately, all we usually teach Brandon is that he had better not get caught the next time, or he will bide his time and wait until he can get back at us in one way or another.

It takes real commitment, perseverance, and courage to discipline your children. It is never easy but always worthwhile. And it pays off. I think of the letter I received from a woman in Chicago. She had a typical problem in her family. Her children wanted too much of her attention. In almost every family there is at least one attention getter— the child who makes a career out of gaining the attention of adults and his peers. Sometimes he does it positively by being well behaved, getting good grades, and so on, but often he does it negatively, and one of his favorite sports is bugging Mom or Dad.

And that's what this lady faced—being bugged, in this case by both of her kids. Her letter mentioned that she had heard me speak at a seminar in Chicago and was particularly interested in my comments about the technique of "pulling the rug out."

Her letter went on to say:

> I was talking with my girlfriend on the telephone and the children were being really obnoxious. I asked them to be quiet at least twice. The third time I remembered what you had said and decided to take action rather than just use words. I put down the phone and escorted the children outside the house. Then I went back to my telephone conversation and talked for at least another twenty minutes.
>
> As I turned from the phone and looked toward the kitchen window, I saw a little hand with a note in it. The note said, "Mommy, we love you—over." Then they flipped the note over and it said, "We are sorry. Can we come in now?"

I remember chuckling with pleasure as I read the mother's letter to me as well as the children's note, which she had included. I sent back my own note, thanking her for sharing her experience with me. I told her she was a brave parent to take that kind of action with her children. And I particularly noted one line in her letter that had said that now when she's on the telephone, her children's behavior is 180 degrees in the other direction. Why the change? Because she took action. She took the little buzzards by the beaks. She told them they could continue to be obnoxious if they wanted to, but if that was their choice they would have to do it outside—especially when Mom was on the telephone.

The moral in this mother's story is crystal clear. Our kids really do notice and pay attention when we take firm action and put reality to work. Yes, it would have been easy for that young mother to give in to her children's pleas as she was trying to put them outside. They probably wailed, "Oh, Mommy! We'll be good. Please don't put us outside. We'll be good."

If that mother had bent at that particular moment, she would have lost the whole battle. But she hung in there and followed through. You can do the same. Never be afraid to pull the rug out and let the little buzzards tumble. I promise you they will land right side up—and so will you!

✔ To Review and Apply

What do you think about spanking? How do you respond to the recommendations in this book?

How can you earn the respect of your children?

✔ To Practice

- *Count your conflicts.* What are the most common battles you fight with your children? Are there issues you keep coming back to? List them.
- *Pull the rug out.* In the common conflicts you've listed, how could you "pull the rug out"? What appropriate measures could you take? Make specific plans.

Six

Danger—Super Parent at Work!

"How can I get my child to like himself better? He seems so unhappy."

"How can I get my child to achieve her potential? I know she can do better."

"How do I get my child to be responsible?"

"I'm worried. I see my kid going in the wrong direction—she's only in the fourth grade and she's already running with the wrong crowd."

"What do we do with Josh? He's already rebelling and we've tried so hard to train him up right, the way God wants."

All of the above comments are typical of what I hear from parents almost every week. These comments reflect parental concern for their children, and I sympathize with every one of them. As a parent, I too have concerns about my own children. I too am bombarded with advice and admonitions on how to do a better job of parenting. There are literally tons of books, articles, pamphlets, tapes, films, and video cassettes out there telling us why and how we should be Super Parent. And I suppose that at several points in this book, I sound just like the rest of the experts:

"Be sure you don't do this. . . . Be sure you do that."

"Be faster than a speeding bullet as you use actions, not words."

"Be more powerful than a locomotive as you enforce the rules of reality discipline."

"Leap tall problems with a single bound, to be loving, caring, and aware of your child's feelings."

I understand when a parent gets frustrated with "advice from the experts." I have felt the same kind of frustrations myself—and I'm supposed to be one of the experts! Parenting *is* a difficult task. My first book on parenting was titled *Parenthood without Hassles—Well, Almost*. While I was confident that parenting could be a much simpler task than a lot of people were making it, I knew *all* the hassles would not disappear.

Now, years later, I am even more realistic. *Making Children Mind without Losing Yours* is the name of the reality discipline game. And quite possibly, by now, you understand that there is one thing wrong with that title: You don't *make* your child mind. By using the concepts of reality discipline, you guide your child toward making wise decisions about the realities of life. And you know you need to give him freedom to fail. Nevertheless, you are positive that he will make more wise decisions than poor ones as he learns to be accountable and responsible by disciplining himself.

What makes what I am saying different from the other "experts"? In some ways, I'm not that different at all. A lot of psychologists and child-rearing specialists believe in discipline, accountability, responsibility, and helping children make wise decisions. But I am convinced that reality discipline has distinctives that need to be practiced in every home where children live.

1. *Parents never seek to punish; they always seek to discipline, train, and teach.*

2. *If "punishment," pain, or some kind of consequence is involved, the parent is not doing it or causing it—reality is.* Your child is learning how the real world works.

3. *Reality discipline is the best system I know to avoid inconsistent meandering between authoritarianism and permissiveness.* Most parents know instinctively that they should be *authoritative*—in charge but reasonable and fair. Staying with the authoritative happy medium is best done through reality discipline.

4. *Reality discipline is the best system for teaching accountability and responsibility in a way that will stick.* The child learns through making his own decisions and experiencing his own mistakes and failures as well as his own successes. He is not a puppet or imitator of his parents; he is their student.

5. *Above all, reality discipline is your best bet for avoiding the Super Parent Syndrome.* When it comes to parenting, most of us not only want to get off the runway but we also want to make our efforts fly—like a bird, like a plane, even like a space capsule. We want our parenting to *work.* We want to be effective. That's why I like to caution parents, "Be a bird, be a plane, but *not* Super Parent!" In fact, if you are using reality discipline concepts at all, they will automatically keep you from making the four key mistakes of a Super Parent.

Pitfalls of the Super Parent Syndrome

The "Big Four" occur in all kinds of homes, but I have found that religious families are particularly susceptible. Super Moms and Super Dads often get trapped into the following four kinds of faulty reasoning:

1. I own my children.
2. I am judge and jury.
3. My children can't fail.
4. I am boss—what I say goes.

All four of these erroneous ideas smack of authoritarianism—the style of parenting that is long on control but short on love and support. The authoritarian parent is "in charge," running things with an infallible and firm hand. It's easy to slip into this kind of thinking when you believe you are doing God's will as you train up your child in the way God wants him to go. Some parents are more authoritarian than others, of course, but it's a role we slip into far too easily, especially if things get out of hand and we get impatient, frustrated, or confused. I believe it's good for parents to be aware of the four pitfalls of the Super Parent Syndrome.

I Own My Children

I believe all parents need to be reminded that they don't own their children. It's true that parenting is a long-term (not to mention expensive) investment. But our children don't belong to us. Reality discipline reminds us that we aren't trying to own or keep our children; we are trying to help them learn to be responsible and accountable persons in their own right.

Our children belong to the Lord. He has given them to us "on loan," with specific guidelines in his Word for the training and enrichment of their lives. When we slip into the Super Parent Syndrome, we can try so hard and get so wrapped up in our children that we try to possess them. And often we can be quite loving while we do it. As I said before, the authoritarian parent is strong on control and short on love and support. That doesn't mean that there aren't many authoritarian homes where there seems to be a lot of love, but it is a benevolent dictatorship. Reality discipline is designed to help you strike a balance that shows your child warmth and love but also gives him freedom to make his own decisions. Reality discipline seeks to guide, not own or control.

I Am Judge and Jury

By the same token, we are not the judge and jury. The only Judge is God himself, and all of us will be judged someday.

Yes, we have authority over our children, but we should always use that authority with tender, loving fairness. Challenges arise every day in our lives and the lives of our children. But reality discipline stresses that we are not to pass down judgments on our children, even though they often try to involve us in doing just that. Children have a natural tendency to see Mom and Dad as infallible and the final court of appeal to help them get what they want at the time. It is often tempting to step in and solve their problems and pronounce the just decree.

For example, let us look in on Ricky and Bobby, ages six and eight. They have been scrapping and fighting after going to bed. Dad has already come in three times and told them to settle down. But Ricky and Bobby keep wrestling, arguing, and carrying on. Finally, Ricky (the six-year-old) starts to cry. That does it—the anger button is pressed inside Dad and off he goes into their room, determined to settle this—now!

"All right! Who started it?" Dad is now judge and jury, and he's going to find out just where he should dispense proper punishment.

For some strange reason, Ricky and Bobby simply point at each other. Dad's judge-and-jury role becomes confusing, so he says, "Now listen up! I've had it. I've told you guys three times to settle down and I mean it! DO YOU UNDERSTAND ME?"

"Yes, Daddy."

"Yes, Daddy."

Dad leaves in anger, slamming the bedroom door so hard it shakes the whole house. And what are Ricky and Bobby doing behind the closed bedroom door? They are looking at each other, hands over mouths, trying to stifle their giggles.

Bobby snickers, "Did you see the veins on his neck? I've never seen him get that mad before."

Meanwhile, Dad returns to the living room to try to continue watching television with Mom. Mom adds to the problem by turning to him to say, "John, it seems to me you were entirely too hard on the boys."

John retorts, "Seems to me if you disciplined around here, I wouldn't have to do that!"

Then Super Mom and Super Dad may go back to watching the news in stony silence, or they may get into a hassle of their own. They have fallen nicely for the strategy of Ricky and Bobby, who have needlessly involved them both in their own little hassle. Ironically enough, while believing he was playing the role of judge and jury, Dad was really being manipulated by his own kids! His first mistake was correcting them three times before they really pressed his button and caused him to commit his second mistake, getting absolutely enraged. His third mistake was asking them, "Who did it?" Of course, neither boy would admit to being guilty.

What should Dad have done? He had several options that could have come out of principles from reality discipline. He could have worked out a "logical consequence" that would have told the boys that if they continued the hassle, they would wind up having to go to bed earlier on the next several nights. Or, he could have removed one child from the bedroom and made him sleep somewhere else for the night. (For more on how to handle this problem, see "Bedtime Battles" in chapter 11.)

Whatever a parent does, he should never play judge and jury. Parents are not running a court. They are operating a home where encouragement takes the place of reward and discipline always triumphs over punishment. It takes a Super Parent to play the judge-and-jury game. You need the speed of a bullet and the strength of a locomotive. To play the reality discipline game, however, you need the wisdom to guide your children in making right decisions and letting reality call the shots.

My Children Can't Fail

When you slip into Super Parent thinking, failure is not a favorable idea. The Super Parent believes he must not and cannot fail because God is on his side. Naturally enough, he believes his children cannot fail either, and if they do fail, he finds this very hard to accept. The feelings of disappointment are interpreted by children as conditional acceptance, and the tension continues to build. The truth is that our children *can* fail.

I believe children should fail on occasion because failure is good for them. Those are bitter words for Super Parents to accept. Several years ago, I was on a radio talk show with Abigail Van Buren of "Dear Abby" fame. Abby had picked up "A Child's Ten Commandments to Parents" from my book *Parenthood without Hassles—Well, Almost* and had printed them in her column. She stated during the talk show that after printing the column she had gotten more than seven hundred letters from people who didn't like one of the commandments, which read: "Please give me the freedom to make decisions concerning myself. Permit me to fail, so that I can learn from my mistakes. Then someday I'll be prepared to make the kind of decisions life requires of me."

Abby's comment was graphic proof of what the problem is in many homes today. Parents are afraid to let their kids fail. I'm not saying that a child should be a failure by habit or that she should learn to be a loser in life. I am saying that we learn through failure. We learn through making our own decisions, and some of those decisions turn out to be mistakes that lead to failure.

No matter how many letters come in criticizing that "seventh commandment," I still believe the home should be a place where failure is allowed. It is dealt with matter-of-factly and is cushioned with love and encouragement from the parents.

I think of Harlan's father, who had been a super athlete in high school and college. Little Harlan tried out for the major division of his Little League team and didn't make it. He was assigned to a minor league team instead. Without Harlan's knowledge or permission, his dad went to the coach and tried to talk about it. In the process, his dad lost his temper and there was a loud shouting match. Some of the parents and most of the team members, all schoolmates of Harlan, heard the whole thing. Harlan was there too and was so embarrassed he didn't want to show his face around school for months. He wound up quitting his minor league team and would have nothing to do with baseball after that.

Failure *is* difficult for parents to deal with. We want our children to succeed in life and be happy, but we need to ask ourselves some questions: When and how did *we* succeed? Didn't we often succeed out of failure? Didn't we come from failure to victory in many phases of our lives?

I think it's interesting that everyone's Christian life begins with failure. When we come to the saving grace of Christ, we do not come out of victory but out of admitting defeat. We are sinners and we need a Savior. As we admit our mistakes and our need of Christ, it is then that we have victory.

I Am Boss—What I Say Goes

The parent who uses reality discipline is in authority but never the boss. In the Christian home, God is boss. The parent is only managing what God has provided. With reality discipline you seek to help your child become accountable and responsible, but you do not make his or her decisions. When you slip into the Super Parent type of thinking, you start making decisions for your children because "you know best."

True, every parent knows more than his or her children (most of the time!). There are many situations where a parent knows what a child should do because the parent has been down that road before.

But reality discipline helps you guide the child, not dominate her and make decisions for her. It is more work to guide a child, but it is infinitely more worthwhile. A parent can make all of his child's decisions, but what happens when the child reaches junior high, high school, college, and adulthood? I often deal with counseling situations that are tragic, and at their base are parents who are still trying to make decisions for grown, or practically grown, children.

Not long ago, I worked with a fifteen-year-old girl I'll call Sarah. She was a teenager whose mom and dad knew exactly what was best for her. The parents totally bottled up Sarah. She had no freedom; she was watched, suspected, not trusted. There was never any evidence that Sarah was rebellious or was doing anything wrong. The parents had no reason not to trust her, but they didn't anyway.

Sarah could go to church, but when there was any kind of outing by the youth groups such as miniature golf, skating, and so on, the parents said a flat no. She never had any dates, not even with a group of her peers.

At age fifteen Sarah turned up in my office—pregnant. She had been climbing out of her window at night to meet a nineteen-year-old boy. The parents had good intentions, but their ignorance of the freedom that children need to learn and to grow caused terrible tragedy. The parents were beside themselves when they finally realized that they had contributed to their daughter's downfall. The girl had always viewed her parents as insensitive and strict. She saw what they did to her as punishment and she said to herself, *Okay, Mom and Dad, if you have the right to punish me, I have the right to punish you.* And she got back at them, only to leave her life in ruins.

I often see parents trying to decide for their children where they will go to school—what college they will attend. Then they decide what job or profession the child should have. Many parents are even involved in deciding whom the child should marry. I'm not saying that parents shouldn't have input about schooling, professions, and marriage partners, but input and opinions are far different from control and pressure.

Then there is that greatest decision of all. Can any parent make his child's decision to accept God in their life? Not even a Super Parent can pull that one off!

The above are just a few examples of how Super Parent thinking leads you down the wrong road every time. Trying to be Super Parent can only cause problems, and if you are a normal family, you already have enough problems to work on. Of course, if you are desperately trying to be Super Parent, you don't like admitting that the problems are there. But there is nothing wrong with having problems. We all have them. The question is, how do we respond to them?

Is Your Family Healthy or Unhealthy?

All families are worried about good health. It's not uncommon for parents to spend thousands of dollars on being sure their families eat properly, get decent medical care, and so on. You can do all that and still have an unhealthy home. The unhealthy part comes from how you, the parents, are responding to the problems that are a part of everyday living. Without trying to push the health analogy too far, I think we can look at problems as we look at germs. Do we let problems infect our families and turn into serious disease? Or can we absorb the problems, fight off the ill effects, and stay healthy?

An instance of unhealthy behavior that I see in quite a few families is their treatment of the "black sheep." Parents will call and make an appointment for family therapy. Then they will bring in little Buford or Cletus and essentially say to me, "Doc, this is the one. This is the one who walks to a different beat. This is the one who rebels against church. This is the one who gets the poor grades. Fix him!"

And the black sheep usually sits there and hangs his head or stares out the window, looking bored to death. My reaction usually surprises the parents. I tell them that if they're going to make any headway in changing Buford's behavior, then they must all consider changing their own behavior first.

Whenever I deal with a family who believes it has a "black sheep" child, I frequently ask the entire family to meet with me. It's important that the family see the misbehavior of one child not as just that child's problem. It is the entire family's problem. Usually there are reasons for the child's behavior, and often the family members are contributing to what is going on.

For example, it's not difficult to miss seeing the payoff a model child gets from having a black-sheep brother or sister a year and a half or so behind him. (Or, perhaps the black sheep is the older child.) Every time the model child does something right, it only makes the black sheep look worse. In many families, the more a model child behaves well, the more she helps destroy the self-esteem and confidence of her black-sheep sibling. The model child would never admit it verbally, but she is definitely getting a payoff out of all this. Her own position in the family is enhanced by the black-sheep brother's or sister's misbehavior. Parents are only human. They do compare and wonder why little Buford can't be like his model older sister.

The question then arises, "All right, what do we do with Buford? Is his model brother or sister supposed to start acting like a black sheep so everyone feels comfortable?"

Of course not, but what families, and especially parents, need to do is look for the purpose behind Buford's temper tantrums, thumb sucking, antisocial behavior, and so on. I try to help parents identify behavior—positive and negative—and then deal with it differently than they have been. The responses by parents and other family members can do much to reinforce unwanted behavior in a child. Likewise, family responses can reinforce desirable behavior. It depends on the response, which can be healthy or unhealthy. The following chart illustrates what I mean. It gives examples of some positive and negative behaviors, healthy and unhealthy parental responses, and the child's perception of himself after each kind of response.

117

Behavior	Unhealthy Parental Response	Child's Perception of Self
Child "forgets" to do his chores and goes off to play with his friends. (Negative)	"You are so irresponsible!" "You will never amount to anything if you don't learn to get your work done." "You're grounded for a week."	"I am bad. I'm not worth much." "I'm being punished and it's not fair."
Child helps Mom wash the dishes and clean up the kitchen. (Positive)	"Here's a dollar for helping Mom." "My, you are such a good boy for helping Mommy."	"Mom likes me as long as I'm good." "I can get money for helping her."
Child is caught cutting classes at school. (Negative)	"How could you do this to us?" "You're a sneak and a liar!" "You'll wind up in reform school."	"I'm no good." "All my parents worry about is how they look to the teachers at school." "I'm going to wind up a punk so I might as well be one."
Child cleans room by herself. (Positive)	"It looks all right but you forgot to hang up your sweater." "You're such a dear for helping Mommy by cleaning your room." "You made God very happy."	"I never do anything right." "Mommy loves me because I cleaned my room." "God only loves me when I do as I'm told."

Healthy Parental Response	Child's Perception
"I really get upset when the chores aren't done. I had to hire the neighbor's boy to do your work. It cost five dollars, and it will be deducted from your allowance." "You won't be going to the scout meeting tonight because you have to stay home and do the chores you didn't do this afternoon."	"Mom is angry because I didn't do my chores." "If I don't do them, I will have to pay the price. She's giving me the choice."
"Thanks for your hard work. I appreciate it." "Having help has made this job a lot easier." "Thank you. The kitchen looks great, doesn't it?"	"I am important. I belong to this family." "I am responsible and I do a good job."
"I'm sorry to hear that you seem to dislike school that much." "Let's talk about it and try to find out what's bugging you." "I could be wrong, but I think you need school, for a lot of reasons."	"My parents are concerned about me." "They want to hear my side."
"Your room looks great." "I'll bet you're proud of your work. Nice job!" "Your effort paid off. What a terrific-looking room!"	"I'm responsible—I can work without Mom being there." "I can discipline myself. I can do it."

The unhealthy parental responses in the two negative examples of behavior are easy to spot. In both cases, the parent sends a "you" message that is loud and clear. It says to the child, in so many words, "You are no good, not worth much, disappointing, and headed for more trouble."

Many children hear this kind of message all the time and instead of improving, they get worse. Parents reinforce the child's negative behavior by telling him he's no good and won't be able to improve. So the child fulfills the prophecy.

Healthier responses to a child when he does something negative are in the form of the "I" message, which lets the child know the parent is hurt, angry, and concerned. But instead of attacking the child, the parent simply shares feelings and concerns and asks the child to work with him to improve the situation.

Now let's take a look at the two samples of positive behavior and the unhealthy and healthy responses. The unhealthy responses are common ones. They may be similar to responses we have gotten from our own parents. For example, "You are such a good boy for helping Mommy."

Now, what's wrong with that? What's wrong with telling the child he's a good boy?

There is quite a bit that is wrong, but it is difficult to spot. The remark conveys that the child is loved *because* he helped Mommy. It implies that he is loved only when he helps. What might be going on in the child's mind when he hears this kind of response? He might be thinking, *What if I didn't help? Wouldn't I be loved?*

While the child may not be able to verbalize it, he might be thinking that the parent's love is conditional. If he doesn't perform, he doesn't get loved. What a parent should always try to convey to any child is that the child is loved whether he helps or not, whether he performs well or not.

Now let's look at the healthy responses: "Having help sure made this job a lot easier"; "Thank you"; and "The kitchen looks great, doesn't it?"

These statements send the child positive messages. The child hears that his work is appreciated. The emphasis is on the job and not on the child. He learns that he made the job easier for his mother and his mother is thankful. This makes him feel good and worthwhile. And then to hear that the "kitchen looks great" lets him know he is capable—that he can do a good job.

The examples on the chart on pages 118 and 119 give you the basic concept of the difference between healthy and unhealthy parental responses to typical problems in the home. Study the chart and think about how healthy your responses to your children usually are. Are you using encouragement and loving discipline, or are you slipping into the unhealthy modes of praise and punishment?

I urge all parents to commit Ephesians 6:4 to memory as a means of continually reminding themselves of the difference between healthy and unhealthy responses to their children. *The Living Bible* says it so well: "Don't keep on scolding and nagging your children, making them angry and resentful. Rather, bring them up with the loving discipline the Lord himself approves, with suggestions and godly advice."

In this single verse, the apostle Paul has painted a perfect portrait of reality discipline. The parent described in Ephesians 6:4 avoids frustrating and dominating his child while attempting to nurture him as God intends. Unfortunately, I see too many moms and dads trying to be Super Parents because they sincerely think this is what Scripture teaches. Ironically enough, these Super Parents depend more on themselves than on God. They may talk about trusting God, but their parenting style reveals that their basic trust is in themselves. They seem to enjoy the role of judge and jury or answer man or lady. They push so hard for excellence that their children are frozen by fear of failure.

And sometimes a Super Parent's striving for excellence can result in wearing that parent out completely while he or she acts as slave or servant to the family. This often happens to mothers. For example, I once counseled Michelle, a perfectionist thirty-four-year-old mother who had three daughters, the oldest in junior high school. Michelle's girls were easy to spot. Their color-coordinated outfits could be seen from more than a block away. Michelle even ironed the bacon for breakfast to be sure it was flat and "neat looking."

When Michelle came to me, she was a thoroughly exhausted woman—physically and emotionally. She was up every morning at 5:30 A.M. She had a battle every day getting the girls out of bed, making sure their teeth were brushed, and so on. At 6:45 A.M., perfectly dressed and groomed, she would serve her family four different breakfasts. One daughter would have blueberry pancakes, another scrambled eggs, and the third cereal. Dad, of course, would usually have his favorite, eggs Benedict.

This idiocy went on day in and day out and finally Michelle started to crack. Her family was a circus and she was trying to be ringmaster. She was an extreme and pathetic illustration of the kind of mother who wants to give her family everything. What she was doing was contrary to sound psychology, common sense, and biblical wisdom. After several weeks of therapy, Michelle finally made some progress. Her most significant act was to finally throw up her hands and announce that she was "going on strike." She did just that, stopped trying to be "Super Mom," and the entire situation improved rapidly.

Ironically, while Michelle believed that she was giving her family love, and while she was certainly trying to act lovingly, she was not achieving her goals at all. By making so many decisions for her children and by constantly "doing for them," she actually hampered their development into responsible persons who could make their own decisions and learn accountability to others, and ultimately to God.

The Ultimate Goal of Reality Discipline

The most important questions parents ask me at the seminars I conduct throughout the United States and Canada are, "How do I help my child develop spiritually? How do I enhance my child's relationship with God?"

I think the key to answering these questions centers around the reality discipline concept of action, not words. Children hear many words about God in their home. They hear many words in Sunday school and church. But they don't always see much action that seems connected to facing God. As they grow older, they often have difficulties with the weakness and hypocrisy of the adults around them. They see the humanness in their parents and others in their homes and churches.

There is nothing wrong with being human, but there is a great deal wrong with being hypocritical. I believe that when I freely admit my humanness to my children, I am taking advantage of an ideal opportunity to teach them dependence upon the grace of God. As I admit to my children that I don't have all the answers and as I pray with them and share with them, they see me depending upon God as I deal with the everyday hassles of life.

One of the best ways to show (not just tell) your children you are truly dependent upon God is through prayer. Do you take time to pray regularly with your children? I'm not talking about sitting on your child's bed just before he goes to sleep and reciting, "Now I lay me down to sleep, I pray this Lord, my soul to keep, like little birdies in their nests, angels guide me while I rest." My children have never heard that kind of prayer. When I pray with them, I want to pray about the day, our needs, about specific problems, whatever they might be. I pray with our children for Grandma or Grandpa, for Mom and Dad, or for brother or sister. I pray with them about something we are particularly thankful for that day—a need that was met or an answer that came.

I also pray with our children about my weaknesses and shortcomings. My children do not hear me thanking God for my perfection. They hear me depending on him for wisdom and strength.

Children look up to adults. Adults are so much bigger and they can do so much more. Adults meet the needs of children throughout the day. It's no wonder that little children actually see their fathers and mothers as "perfect."

Of course, the mantle of perfection soon drops in tatters from our shoulders. But as long as we have children fooled, we are not doing them any favors with our masquerade. Perfect people cause others to be uncomfortable, and they are not easy to be around. They don't seem that approachable, and if there's anything I want to be as a parent to my children, it is approachable.

It is sad to see so many parents—out of pride or selfishness—refuse to let their children know that they have flaws and that they don't have it all together. When parents are brave enough to share their flaws and lacks with their children through prayer, they serve as beautiful models of what it means to depend on God. When you are open and transparent before God and your children, you are saying that, "even though I am many years older, I too depend on our heavenly Father, just as I want you to depend on him."

Another benefit of being open before God and your children is that it will motivate them to seek you out and talk about their real feelings. They are more likely to share their problems and weaknesses with you, if they know that you have been down that same road yourself. They will reason, *Mommy won't be mad about this because she had it happen, too.*

I think prayer time is the most special time of the day for you and your children. I urge you to hold your children as you pray. Take your time and don't hurry. Really speak from the heart. Stay away from cute prayers and prayers that you can memorize. Teach your children to pray from the heart and teach them to pray for their every need.

Show your child that you are depending on the all-encompassing love and strength of God in your life. Model submission to the Lord before your child and he will learn how to submit his own life to God.

Make prayer a priority in your home, along with going to church and Sunday school. Take time to have devotions around the dinner table. Take every opportunity to have the courage to share your innermost thoughts and feelings about your heavenly Father. Your children will learn to do the same.

I believe that modeling submission to God results in a double blessing: (1) you take definite steps toward your ultimate goal—to guide your child to make his own decisions, especially the decision to accept Christ as Lord of his life; and (2) you fulfill your role of the authoritative parent, which Paul describes in Ephesians 6:4. Note, I said *authoritative,* not *authoritarian.* The authoritative parent stands on the solid middle ground between the extremes of permissiveness and authoritarianism. As the chart on page 127 describes, neither the permissive or the authoritarian parent helps the child learn to make decisions. The permissive parent robs the child of self-respect and a sense of initiative by doing so much *for* her. The authoritarian parent robs the child of self-esteem and a sense of independence by doing so much *to* her.

The authoritarian parent controls the child with autocratic rule, but such despotism is doomed to ineffectiveness. The autocratic authoritarian may think his child is "toeing the mark," but in actuality this parent has made himself accountable for the child's behavior. Authoritarianism invites rebellion because it fosters two kinds of behavior in the child. One kind is for the parents and other authority figures to see. The other kind is what the child does when on his own or out with his friends. Believe me, these behaviors can be radically different.

One of the laments I hear almost every week is, "Little Festus is one way at home, but when he's with his friends, he's always in trouble."

When I can identify a parent's style as autocratic and authoritarian, I gently ask, "What can you expect? You have deprived your child of the opportunity to make decisions about life. You have been emphasizing control but neglecting to teach him to be independent and self-confident in his own decisions."

I believe the home should be a place where children can learn to make decisions about their lives and learn to accept the consequences of their decisions—the good and the bad. The home is really a tuition-free university where children study the lifelong curriculum of decision making. I say free because God has given us free will. We can make our own decisions, including whether or not to accept or reject his offer of eternal love and salvation. The freedom we have is one of the great proofs of how much God loves us.

The home ought to be a reflection of that kind of love. God is in authority over the parents but gives them freedom and love. The parents are in authority over the children, and the children should also have freedom and love.

This sounds dangerous to some parents. They keep grasping the concept of control. If they do not control their child, he will get out of hand, he will get hurt, he will go the wrong way, and so on. But if you stop to think, the parent has no other real choice than to give his child freedom. I'm not saying he should neglect his child or let him run into the street and get killed. But at the base of the child-parent relationship should be the parent's desire to train the child, guide her, and set her free to become her own person. The child is becoming an individual anyway, and instead of cramping and crimping the process, you should encourage it and enhance it.

The Authoritarian Parent	The Authoritative or Responsible Parent	The Permissive Parent
1. Makes all decisions for the child.	1. Gives the child choices and formulates guidelines with him or her.	1. Is a slave to the child.
2. Uses reward and punishment to *control* child's behavior.	2. Provides the child with decision-making opportunities.	2. Places priority on the child, not on his or her spouse.
3. Sees himself as *better than* the child.	3. Develops consistent, loving discipline.	3. Robs the child of self-respect and self-esteem by doing things for him that the child can do for himself.
4. Runs the home with an iron hand; grants little freedom to the child.	4. Holds the child accountable.	4. Provides the child with the "Disney-land" experience; makes things as easy as possible—does homework for the child, answers for the child, and so on.
	5. Lets reality be the teacher.	5. Invites rebellion with inconsistent parenting.
	6. Conveys respect, self-worth, and love to the child and therefore enhances the child's self-esteem.	

Your child will soon be an adolescent and then an adult. She will soon do what she wants anyway (and this comes much sooner than you think). Even as early as the teenage years, we basically don't have a lot to go on but our child's love and respect. We may think we have power and control, but it is fast slipping away.

I deal with parents all the time who have not granted freedom to their children, and they are now reaping bitter fruit as the children become teenagers and young adults. The entire thrust of this book is to help you train up your child from his earliest years to make wise decisions. You can have no greater goal as a parent.

✔ To Review and Apply

Have you ever tried to be a Super Parent? How? What have the results been?

What were the four lines of faulty reasoning for the Super Parent? Which of these are you most susceptible to?

✔ To Practice

- *Stop being perfect.* You're not, anyway, so you can stop pretending. Give up some unreasonable task you're trying to accomplish for your family. Or admit a shortcoming.
- *Pray with your children.* Show your children that you rely on prayer daily. Don't preach, just let the reality of God's presence into your home. Be honest about your relationship with God and encourage your kids to be honest too.

Seven

The Way to Be Your Child's Best Friend

So far, we have looked at some basic principles behind reality discipline. These concepts include the following:

Reality disciplinarians try to be consistent, decisive, and respectful of their children as persons.

Reality disciplinarians use guidance rather than force, but they are action-oriented, not satisfied to just use words.

Reality disciplinarians hold their children accountable for their actions, whatever those actions are, to help their children learn from experience. That experience may include failure or success, but in all cases the children are responsible and accountable for what they do.

Reality disciplinarians are concerned about helping their children learn. They realize they are the most important teachers their children can ever have, but they also seek the best possible school situations for their children.

Perhaps you cringe a bit when I use the term *reality disciplinarian*. Our normal concept of a disciplinarian is someone who is strict, authoritarian, and generally not too much fun to live with. What I'm hoping to do in this book, however, is to show you that by being a disciplinarian, you will be the best friend your child ever had. A disciplinarian is someone who guides, trains, and teaches to help another person become more mature, responsible, and successful in life.

Reject the Behavior, Love the Child

And the bottom line is that children want discipline. They will not reject you because you are a disciplinarian as long as they are sure you are not rejecting them. And that is the beauty of the reality discipline concept. Reality discipline allows parents to communicate to their children that they love them even though they don't always love their behavior. My practice in counseling, along with the seminars I conduct all over the country, shows me again and again that parents are unskilled in the art of helping their children see that, "I love you but I don't like what you did." Somehow the children continue to get the message that, "you don't like what I did and you don't like me very much either."

But the children keep coming back for more. They keep testing and rebelling and probing and all the time they are asking one basic question: "Do you love me? Do you love me enough to discipline me and correct me, but at the same time, do you still like me?"

Balance is a key word when using reality discipline. The child misbehaves and you must deal with it. If you deal with it in too permissive a manner, the child will soon decide that he is running the house. If you deal with it with too much of the authoritarian approach, the child will feel that you are trampling him and bide his time until he can get back at you in one way or another. "Getting back" can run the gamut from being sassy or disobedient, all the way to running away or suicide. The tragedy that I see repeatedly happening is rebellious children who literally destroy their lives as they seek to retaliate against parental authoritarianism.

Some children reared in authoritarian homes remain "good little boys and girls" until they reach upper adolescence or early adulthood, and then they get their revenge through open rebellion, rejection of their faith, and so on. And I have counseled many adults who don't rebel until later in life. Many a "mid-life crisis" is a man or a woman working out feelings about an authoritarian upbringing.

Always Keep Short Accounts

Reality discipline seeks to not be too permissive and not be too authoritarian. You try to be consistent and always action-oriented. A parent using reality discipline keeps short accounts. There isn't a lot of saving up of resentment or anger or frustration. When a rule is broken or another kind of misbehavior occurs, the child knows that there will be an immediate settlement of the situation.

And a "settlement" does not necessarily mean an immediate swat or spanking. There is a place for corporal punishment but I believe too many parents use it when they don't have to. The key issue in any situation that calls for discipline is that the child sees what she did wrong, that she has an opportunity to repent and feel sorry, and that she feels that she's been dealt with fairly.

In some cases a child may feel truly sorry and express his repentance to the offended person. If the child has asked for forgiveness, he should be forgiven. What is important is

131

to communicate. If possible, the child and his mother or father should talk about the situation. It is during this time of talking about a misbehavior or a breaking of rules that real training takes place. With reality discipline you are not disciplining your child simply for the sake of disciplining him or even for the sake of "keeping order." Your long-range goal is to help your child become an accountable and responsible person who learns how to discipline himself.

Use Your Most Powerful Ally

As you train your child with reality discipline, always make good use of your most powerful ally: natural or logical consequences. The concept of "natural consequences" was first developed by psychiatrist Rudolf Dreikurs. Dreikurs believed that the best way to train children is to let life do the work. Many consequences are "natural" in that they will simply happen if events are left to take their course. The Scripture nicely describes natural consequences in Galatians 6:7. To paraphrase the verse slightly, "A child reaps what he sows." For example:

Run when you should walk and you slip and scrape your knee.

Stay up too late and be late for school the next day.

"Logical" consequences are a little different. The parents set logical consequences up ahead of time by talking to the child about what will happen if certain responsibilities are not met. For example:

Refuse to eat your dinner, and it goes in the garbage (or to Bowser) and you get nothing to eat until breakfast.

Come home late from your friend's house and you can't go there tomorrow (or you have to come home sooner the next time).

Repeatedly forget to feed the cat and we have to find a new home for the cat.

As you use natural or logical consequences with your child, be willing to explain things but don't go over and over the ground rules and don't give a lot of warnings, extra chances, and so on. One of your key goals is to teach your child that consequences in life are real and life doesn't always give a second chance.

Daily living gives you constant opportunities to put natural or logical consequences into action. And every time you do, be ready for that critical "moment of truth" when the consequence has to occur. If you weaken or become too permissive, your discipline will lack reality and results.

Remorse Can Be a Child's Weapon

As a parent, I realize it isn't always easy to hang tough and enforce logical or natural consequences. It can be downright painful to let natural consequences take their course as you let little Buford sleep in and he is late for school. There will be wails, tears, and remorse, all of which can be nerve-racking.

I often caution parents to be aware that their child's remorse can be real or possibly a manipulative weapon. If your child is continually breaking the same rule or doing the same thing wrong and continuing to show remorse, he may be using it as a weapon. He may be learning that, *as long as I tell Mommy I'm sorry, I can get away with it.* Keep in mind that reality discipline always asks for accountability. Remorse is good, but in many cases it is not enough. For example, when a child breaks something in a home through violating a direct rule such as "no rough-housing," he may show a great deal of remorse. But he's also to be held accountable for what he broke.

133

The same principle of accountability would hold true for a child who is continually late for dinner. You might accept his apology on one or two occasions, but if the behavior continues, the child will have to wind up not having any dinner.

I remember a nine-year-old young lady I was working with in a number of counseling sessions. She was eagerly looking forward to spending a certain weekend with her girlfriend. She was going to stay overnight at the girlfriend's house, have breakfast the next morning, and then go on a special outing with her friend's mother.

But our nine-year-old young miss also had a number of chores that had to be done each week by Friday evening. All the chores were predetermined and the time limits were clearly set by Mom.

Friday rolled around and at 6:30 P.M. the daughter reminded Mom that now was the time to go to her girlfriend's house. The only problem was that her chores were not finished. In fact, most of them weren't even started. Mom calmly said, "Honey, I'm sorry, but you're not going to be able to go."

Naturally there were tears and a scene, but after things calmed down, the daughter returned to the table, still teary-eyed, and said, "But Mommy . . . why?"

Mother calmly said, "Honey, because the chores that you were to do after school today weren't done. I'm sorry, but you're going to have to stay home this evening and finish those chores."

What happened next is interesting and most significant to parents who are interested in using reality discipline. With all the skill and wisdom that children seem to possess, the nine-year-old daughter started chastising her mother.

"But Mom . . . you didn't tell me I had to do this! How come you didn't warn me?"

See how easy it is to create a monster—if you please, a "little buzzard"? Our children are so adept at holding us at bay and making us feel guilty. They have any number of ways of communicating to us that we have to warn them and cajole them and coax them and even bribe them. All of that is nonsense! The daughter had been clearly told what her chores were and what the time limits were. What Mother had never done before was to firmly enforce the rules.

And here is where the rubber meets the road in reality discipline. You will come to that moment when you have to enforce the rules and there will be tears and there will be accusations and chastisement. You can either shrink into a shell of guilt and permissiveness and relent or you can don your armor of authoritarianism. Neither will help.

What you have to do is what this mother did. She was calm but still determined. She was firm but still affectionate. Of course, she wasn't number one on her nine-year-old's popularity poll over that weekend. But she was more interested in teaching accountability than she was in copping out with permissiveness in order to get daughter to "like her." And that's what the teaching of accountability takes—sometimes we have to pull the rug out and let the little buzzards tumble.

Effective reality discipline is centered around the concept of controlling your emotions rather than having your emotions control you. This is obviously easier to say (or for me to write) than to do when the window is broken, or the vase has shattered on the floor. It's not always that easy to control one's emotions when little Courtney comes in late with a smart-alecky attitude, or you find four-year-old Cletus bathing his two-year-old sister in the toilet. Nonetheless, to blow up solves nothing. In fact, on those occasions when we do overreact and do not discipline in love, we owe it to our children to go to them and ask their forgiveness. This may be difficult, but it is a powerful tool to model the teachings of Christ to "forgive as the Lord forgave you" (see Eph. 4:32 and Col. 3:13).

In any situation, it is up to you, the parent, to evaluate what's going on and what the best approach will be. The key to interacting effectively with your children is to think before you discipline. I realize that is not always so simple, especially when reality discipline calls for decisive action and not stalling around. But in any situation, it never hurts to take a few moments to think through exactly what is going on and what needs to be done. By taking time out (if necessary, remove yourself or your children from the immediate situation), you decrease the probability of acting only in anger and you increase the probability of administering effective discipline.

Nine Ways to Be Your Child's Best Friend

In summary, here are nine principles to remember when using reality discipline to be your child's best friend:

1. The discipline should fit the infraction. For example, the child misuses her allowance. When she asks for something extra before the week is out, you simply say, "Sorry, you will have to use your allowance and if you haven't any left, you will have to wait until Saturday."
2. Never beat or bully your child into submission. Remember, the shepherd's rod was used to guide the sheep, not to wale them.
3. Use action-oriented methods whenever possible.
4. Always try to be consistent.
5. Emphasize order and the need for order. Work comes before play, chores come before breakfast, and so on. This concept reinforces obedience and emphasizes that in all of God's kingdom, there is a need for order—order is important.
6. Always require your child to be accountable and responsible for his or her own actions.
7. Always communicate to your child that he or she is good, even though the behavior may have been irresponsible.

8. Always give your child choices that reinforce cooperation but not competition.

9. If spanking is necessary, it should be done when you're in control of your emotions. It should *always* be followed up with explanations for why the spanking was necessary, and those all-powerful words, "I love you and I care about you."

It's Simple, but Effective

I have had more than one parent say to me, "You're really asking an awful lot. I have difficulty disciplining my child with your methods."

I tell these parents that I empathize. Reality discipline is a simple, straightforward approach, but it *is* difficult. It is not easy to be like the mother of the nine-year-old who failed to do her chores. The little girl neglected her responsibilities and could not go to her friend's house for the evening. She tried every trick she knew to make Mom feel guilty, but Mom hung in there. She was firm but still affectionate. She was understanding but still steadfast, *and she held her child accountable.*

There is nothing particularly unique about holding your child accountable. Many child-rearing specialists suggest this. But I like to believe that reality discipline is an especially effective way to do it because of the emphasis on being action-oriented, being willing to "pull the rug" with good humor but immovable determination. And it's worth it. Reality discipline works! I see it work every day in my own home. I see it work in the families I counsel and speak to across the country. In part two of this book we will look at some specific problems, hassles, and concerns to see how reality discipline can improve and strengthen your relationship to your children—starting now.

✔ To Review and Apply

This chapter says, "By being a disciplinarian, you will be the best friend your child ever had." How can that be?

What are "natural" and "logical" consequences? Why are these important in disciplining your child?

✔ To Practice

Find truth in consequences. Think about some natural and logical consequences you can use to discipline your child appropriately. Plan your policies.

Eight

When the Nuclear Family Explodes

Gail was a single mom struggling to bring up two young sons, but when her church sponsored a child-rearing seminar, she didn't come. The next Sunday, her pastor asked her why. "Maybe you already have all the answers," he teased her gently.

"Oh, no, Pastor. You know better than that," she replied. "But when I saw all those posters with both parents together, and when you kept announcing the seminar being for moms and dads, I guess I figured it wasn't for me. It's kind of different when you're alone."

Too often we authors and speakers make it sound as if our child-rearing advice is only for two-parent situations— "nuclear families," as the sociologists call them. Many single parents feel left out, as if our carefully tested formulas must be applied in perfectly balanced, hermetically sealed laboratories, and their own lopsided families just don't make the grade. If I've made it sound like that in this book, I'm sorry. The truth is, single parents can apply reality discipline just as effectively as anyone. For many, it may be just what they need.

Studies show that nearly 30 percent of the children in the United States now live in single-parent homes. About another 20 percent live in stepfamilies, or what I call "blended families." *Ozzie and Harriet* are giving way to *The Brady Bunch* and *Murphy Brown*. Nuclear families are exploding, and many have to live with the fallout.

How does reality discipline apply in these situations? Are there special ways of showing love and firmness, of "pulling the rug out," of holding kids accountable, when you're the only parent in the home, or when you're raising someone else's children? Yes and no. Most of the rest of this book still holds true in those cases, but there are some additional considerations, which we'll cover here.

Single-Parent Homes

The hardest job in the world is to be a single parent. You are breadwinner and bread baker, guide and gorilla, nurse and nag. You are single-handedly taking on the two-person task of parenting, in addition to whatever other jobs and activities you have. Most of the single parents I know are just plain weary.

Most single-parent situations are created through loss—the loss of a spouse and parent through death or divorce. Great pain goes along with both these cases, and sometimes guilt or anger. So not only do you struggle to cope with your everyday life, you also have a stewpot of emotions to deal with—yours and your children's! It's not an easy life. (I recognize that increasing numbers of never-married women are choosing motherhood. The emotions may be somewhat different in these cases, but it's still not easy.)

Are you doomed, then, to a second-rate life? Will your children be forever scarred by this situation? Not necessarily. I know many children of single parents who are responsible teenagers and adults, happy, productive, and well-adjusted. That's testimony to their character, their parent's hard work, and the grace of God.

Take Care of Yourself

If you're a single parent with custody of your kids, your life is full of stress. I mean, your stress levels are off the chart. There are always ten million things to do and time for only twelve or thirteen. If it's not your boss asking you to work late, it's your kids wanting a ride to the mall, or the bank calling about a late loan payment. It's always something.

Many in high-stress lives learn to hum along at a rapid pace. They get so used to it, they don't even notice how stressed they are. Often it takes some kind of breakdown—emotional, physical, or relational—to let them know. Don't wait for that to happen. Be aware of your own stress levels and do what you can to ease them now.

First of all, be sure to cover the basics—rest, food, and exercise. Get your seven or eight hours of sleep a night and eat three square meals a day. Avoid snack foods but also fad diets. If you can't get out to a gym go play with your kids, but find some regular time to be active.

Then tackle your schedule. There will be lots of things you just don't have time to do. As a single parent, you can't be a joiner. Learn to say no when people ask you to do time-consuming things. If you're a people-pleaser this is murder, but if you don't it might be suicide. Recognize that you can't do it all.

Take time-outs in your high-stress times. Monitor when you feel especially stressed and take appropriate measures so you don't go through the roof. Maybe it's a time of day when you always feel stressed, or a particular task, someone you talk with, or something your kids do. In any case, moderate your stress levels by pulling back a little, taking a mental mini vacation.

Try to get your kids to help you cope. I know one mom who declared that the first half-hour after she got home was "quiet time." She was not to be disturbed. After that, she would tend to her children's needs cheerfully, but she needed that thirty minutes of down time. Her kids learned that their lives were much sweeter when they gave mom that time off. You need some time like that too. Let your kids know that sometimes *your* needs come first.

Pamper yourself a little. Find small indulgences that make you feel like a million bucks even if they cost seven-fifty. Get dinner delivered, get a pedicure, take a warm bath, go to a concert with friends. Budget some time and money for your own simple pleasures and don't feel guilty about it.

What does all this have to do with reality discipline? It's a starting point. You need to be a strong entity in the family to make this work, and that means you need to take care of yourself. Earlier I said that a parental couple ought to get a good baby-sitter and get away from the kids every so often. They need to keep their relationship strong in order to be good parents. The same thing is true with you, except there's only one of you right now. Take some time to keep yourself strong. And get away from the kids once in a while.

Understand Your Children's Pain but Don't Indulge It

Obviously you're not the only one who's hurting. Your children are hurting too. This pain will be there for a long time, though it will slowly fade away. In the first two years the pain will pop up in many surprising ways, and for a few years thereafter it will continue to make guest appearances.

Sometimes your children will lash out in anger. If you're nearby, they will lash out at you. (That's the thing about anger; it's not always picky about its target.) Some children will close up, refusing to display emotion. Some will seem self-destructive. Some will stop working at school. Some will just refuse to do anything you ask.

How can you discipline a child for feeling hurt? You know what he or she is going through, and you sympathize. In fact, you might even feel a bit guilty for causing that pain (and guilt is the propellant for most of the bad decisions a single parent can make). You might want to compensate for their loss by giving your kids too many second chances or by not saying no.

But that won't really help them. Certain behavior is still unacceptable. You need to expect your child—even a hurting child—to contribute to the well-being of the family. You're all in this together, and you have to help one another. You are all feeling pain, but that's no excuse for destructive actions. More than ever, you need to show love for your misbehaving child ("I understand") while still requiring the child to act properly. If you want to give your kid something to compensate for the pain, just be a consistent, loving parent with healthy standards.

Let Your Children Know You Are Committed to Them . . . Forever

Especially in cases of divorce, children fear further abandonment. They have learned that they can't trust an adult they loved. That might come out in a hesitancy to trust you, or to show love to anyone. Since reality discipline is based on mutual commitment—each individual family member contributing to the whole—this could make things tricky.

Do all you can to keep the sense of family, whether you have one child or eleven. You need to commit yourselves to one another. As the remaining parent, you bear the burden of proof. You need to convince your children that you're there for the long haul. You will not bail when things get tough. It may take time to break down their emotional defenses, and that will be frustrating for you, but keep telling them you're there for them. Keep declaring your commitment.

Follow Your Game Plan Regardless of Your Ex

Once you decide to implement reality discipline, stick with it—even if your ex doesn't go along. Let your kids know that you have "house rules." When they stay with you, there are certain expectations. If they visit the other parent on certain weekends, they can follow other rules. But in your home, they follow your guidelines.

"But Daddy lets me do this!"

"That's fine, when you're with Daddy. But here you can't."

Your children may complain for a while, but soon they'll get the hang of it. They may even taunt you by saying they like the other parent more. Don't fall for this. Stick with your plan of reality discipline as long as your kids are in your keeping.

Of course it helps to present a somewhat united front to your children even if you're divorced. If you're on fairly good terms with your ex, especially where the children are concerned, you could describe your reality discipline methods to your former spouse and hope that he or she might go along. Explain what your expectations are for each of the children and how you hold them accountable. For the good of the children, your ex might agree to support your style of discipline.

But that's not necessary. People often misunderstand reality discipline, considering it a bit too harsh, and your ex may worry that you're being too hard on the kids. Don't let this deter you. Stay with your game plan.

Avoid Triangle Relationships

Say your ex-husband arranges to pick up your son at 10 A.M. Saturday for a day at an amusement park. Your little boy is all dressed and packed and sitting on the front stoop by 9:45. Ten o'clock rolls by, then 10:30, then 11:00—no dad. Your weepy child drags in and says, "Why isn't he coming? He promised."

Of course you're sizzling right now. He was never good at keeping promises and now it's agony to see your son so disappointed. You're reaching for the phone already, burning to give your ex a piece of your mind.

But it's not your problem. Seriously, this is between your ex and your boy. You don't have to get involved. Hand the phone to your son and say, "I don't know. You know his number. Ask him."

Not only do you stay out of an explosive situation, but your child can learn a valuable lesson, though a painful one. And which voice on the line will have more effect on the absentee father—your shrill scolding or your son's plaintive pleas? Let your child have his own relationship with the other parent.

Often children of divorce are pressed into service as carrier pigeons or stool pigeons. As they shuttle back and forth between their parents, they carry messages (usually unpleasant ones) or they gather information.

"Tell that no-good father of yours to bring you back at a reasonable hour this time."

"Is your mother seeing anyone these days?"

If you have business with your ex, do it directly or go through lawyers. Don't put your kids in the middle. Also avoid the temptation to try to win your children's primary allegiance. Sometimes divorced parents find a certain victory in the idea that "the kids like me more." As a result, they bad-mouth the other parent whenever possible. This is unhealthy for the children, who must learn to respect both parents as much as possible. (Also, your desire to be liked by your children may sabotage your reality discipline. If your kids are pawns in some emotional game, they can quickly learn to use that as leverage against you. "Dad's nicer than you. He doesn't make me go to bed till eleven!")

Sometimes your kids or your ex will try to draw you into the middle of their relationship. "Why doesn't Daddy love me more?" "I think Tyler is mad at me these days. Why?" Sure, you want to be helpful, but the middle is a dangerous place to be. Encourage direct communication as much as possible.

Don't Be a Problem-Solver

As a single parent, you get used to single-handedly meeting your child's needs. That can quickly evolve into a protective spirit, which makes you want to shield your child from reality. In addition, single parents often feel great guilt for putting their children in this less-than-perfect situation, and that makes them want to compensate by protecting their little ones from any additional suffering.

But the key to reality discipline is that children must learn to face reality, and sometimes (as they say) "reality bites." I know it's hard to watch your kid get a zero in history class because she chose to watch TV rather than do her report, but that doesn't mean you should do it for her. She will make a better choice next time. It's tough to see your son get cut from the school soccer team, but that doesn't mean you should call the coach and complain. Your son will work harder next year—or maybe find another area of interest that suits his talents better.

Reality really is a good teacher, though often a harsh one. And you don't do your kids any favors by protecting them from it. Fight the temptation to solve all their problems. Let them discover some reality on their own.

Don't Lean Too Much

Single parents often try to get children to assume some of the responsibilities of the former spouse. That's fine if it's just taking out the trash. But if you're using a child as an emotional confidant, watch out. This is especially true if you have only one child. It becomes "You and Me against the World." It's tempting to pour out your soul to your child on a regular basis.

But this can break down reality discipline by undermining your "healthy authority." If you're a soul mate one minute, it's hard to be a disciplinarian the next. I'm not saying you shouldn't be honest with your children and enjoy their company. You should! But remember that you're still a parent.

And remember that your kid is just a kid. Many of your feelings are "adult" in nature—complex, conflicted. Your child isn't ready for all that. *You* may feel great after unburdening yourself to your listening child, but now the child is bearing your burdens and may crumble underneath that load. If you're worried about money, musing about your love life, or ranting about your ex—keep it to yourself or (better yet) find another adult to talk with.

If you have several children, you'll probably lean on the oldest to help with the younger ones. Nothing wrong with that—Sande and I have done that often (though the wide range of our children's ages makes that easy). But be careful about dumping too much responsibility on the oldest child. He or she must not become a "co-parent" with you. Allow some natural leadership to emerge in that child, but keep the parental responsibility to yourself.

Avoid the Grandparent Trap

I counseled one single mom, thirty-five years old, with two children, ages twelve and ten. Her parents decided to take them all to Disney World and made all the arrangements, paying for the whole trip. This was a wonderful gift, but the single mom felt ambivalent about it. I agreed with her. This gift was nice but also dangerous.

Essentially the grandparents were acting as parents. They were deciding things for their adult daughter and her children. On this trip *they* would be in charge, not her. And what would her children learn from that?

Maybe you wouldn't mind an all-expenses-paid trip to Disney World right now. That could be a good thing, except these grandparents were inadvertently using that to exert power over their daughter and her kids. I believe they felt somewhat guilty about her three divorces—they must not have raised her right. And now they weren't trusting her to raise her children right, so they were taking charge. (In fact they had already been caring for the kids occasionally for two to three weeks at a time while their daughter needed a break.)

The grandparents were being nice but also controlling. And the daughter was letting that happen. When people keep doing things for you, pretty soon you get the message you can't do it on your own.

I suggested that the best thing for this family was for the daughter to take the role of parent and for the grandparents to support her in that. The Disney trip would not support her parenthood (but if they really wanted to help, they could give *her* the money and let her take her kids).

That story could be retold about many single-parent homes. Grandparents, often saddled with a vague guilt and usually sincerely desiring to help, usurp the role of the parent. The single parent, who's struggling as it is, lets it happen. But this is a trap, undermining the proper lines of authority in the family. Single parents and their parents need to cooperate to bolster the respect between parent and child. Grandparents need to help without controlling.

Be Careful about Your Love Life

Since the divorce or death that made you a single parent, there's been a huge hole in your life. Naturally, you'd like to find someone to fill it. But you need to be careful when your heart starts latching onto people. Are you falling in love or falling in need? In the wake of a tragedy, you're a very needy person, and that will cause an imbalance in any new relationship. The experts say it takes at least two years to heal emotionally from a divorce, often more. If you get involved with someone else too soon, you're setting yourself up for another fall.

But you want to be especially careful about your children. Granted, much of your sense of need is based on your children's need for a father or mother. You recognize that single parenting is tough for everyone involved, and you fantasize that a new spouse would solve all these problems. But glance over the next few pages and you'll see that starting a stepfamily ain't no picnic either. To marry the wrong person—again—would do even more damage to your family. So go slowly.

Your children are harboring many of the same fantasies you are. They see you chatting with a friendly checkout clerk at the Acme and they're already planning the wedding. If you bring a date around, you can bet they're checking out this person as a potential mom or dad. As part of their grieving process, they hang onto the idea that the damage can be undone. When they finally realize that you and your ex are history, they look for someone else to fill that role to make everything like it used to be. Of course it never works that way. You can't go back. The only way through this is forward. Still, that backward pressure from the kids is liable to crack a new relationship.

I recommend that you keep your love life private as much as possible. Don't share details of your dates with your children and don't bring your dates around the house until you're engaged. That would just set up your kids for disappointment. The best way to be healthy as a family (and as an individual) is to accept the idea that you may remain single, and you have to learn to cope as a family without that missing piece. That's reality. Then if God does bring a new spouse into your life, you'll be entering the relationship that much stronger.

Connie met Rick through friends at work, and they began dating. With two boys from a marriage that had ended two years earlier, she was ready for a serious relationship. Rick seemed like the perfect guy for her. Even her father, who had never liked any man she had ever been with, approved heartily when she brought Rick around.

When Rick took her sons fishing, Connie fell even more in love. At nine and eleven, Jake and Jeffy really needed a father figure—and Rick was the kind of outdoorsman they looked up to. In fact, the whole family was crazy about Rick. They made a cozy group.

But then Connie started to notice some problems. Mysterious business trips. Excuses that didn't quite add up. At first she shrugged them off, but soon she realized that Rick was cheating on her. When she finally confronted him, he laughed. "Oh, that. Hey, I'm a guy. It's not like we're married or anything. It's no big thing."

Of course it was a big thing to her. She had already been zooming toward marriage in her mind, but now she slammed on the brakes. Her ex-husband was a cheater. She wasn't going to let that happen again.

Jake and Jeffy were sad that they wouldn't see Rick again. Connie delicately explained the situation, but they had practically adopted Rick as a father. They ended up blaming Connie for the breakup, displaying a rebellious attitude that poisoned their home for months to come.

That made Connie's life even worse. Naturally, she was suffering from Rick's betrayal, and now she had to fight her kids every day. She worried that she wasn't appealing enough to hold Rick's interest. Why would he need to see other women? And she felt guilty for raising her children's hopes and then dashing them. This hodgepodge of emotions made her very needy, and that need drove her into the arms of another man.

Stan was new to the community, new to her church, good-looking but never married. He wasn't the macho man that Rick was, but he was steady, serious about his goals, holding a good job in an insurance company with room to rise. Connie hit it off well with Stan, showing him around the town, helping him fix up his apartment. He needed her and she needed him. Exactly four months after the debacle with Rick, Connie had her first official date with Stan.

Soon he was eating dinner with Connie and her kids three nights a week. Jake and Jeffy were wary about him, but they got used to having him around. Eventually they kind of liked him, especially when he helped with their homework. Connie began to think that the relationship just might work out this time. Stan, she felt, was definitely marriage material, the kind of guy who could take care of her and her boys.

After six months of steady dating, Connie was getting restless. She wanted to push the relationship to the next level, but Stan seemed content where it was. She realized that she was taking all the initiative in getting together, as if he really didn't care whether they saw each other or not. How does a great guy like that get to be thirty-seven years old without marrying? Maybe he has a problem with commitment.

Connie decided to tackle the issue head on. One night in her living room, she turned off the TV and talked about her desire to be married again. They didn't need to rush into it, she assured Stan, but she definitely wanted to head in that direction. In response, he hemmed and hawed and was generally . . . noncommittal.

She never saw him again. He stopped calling. He left the church. He wouldn't return her calls. She had pushed him too far, and he ran away from the relationship.

Jake and Jeffy didn't show a lot of emotion this time, but over the next year their behavior took a major turn for the worse. Their grades plummeted. Jeffy was getting in fights at school. One day Connie got a call from the police station: Jake had been picked up for shoplifting.

The cycle of heartbreak was bad enough for Connie, but she pulled her kids through it too. They didn't know how to handle the disappointment and the resulting anger. Their emotions seeped out in many destructive ways.

Connie's story is repeated often. I've counseled scores of families with similar sagas of dashed hopes and reopened wounds. That's why I tell single parents to treat their kids with kid gloves when it comes to new romances. Obviously you need to be very careful with your own heart in your time of need, but be especially protective of your children. Don't strap them with you in the roller coaster of love.

My best advice to single parents is: (1) Don't date; (2) if you do, meet outside your home; and (3) don't bring him (or her) around until there's something on your (or her) left hand that cuts glass.

As you'll see in the next chapter, even when new relationships are successful, they often cause more problems than they solve.

✔ To Review and Apply

How can you understand your children's pain without indulging them? Why is this important?

What have been your biggest challenges as a single parent?

Which of the suggestions for this chapter seem hardest for you to follow? Which seem easiest? Why?

✔ To Practice

Make a plan to put into practice the hardest suggestion you just mentioned and the easiest. Be specific about meetings, conversations, policies, people, etc.

Nine

Families Don't Blend, They Collide

Parents used to have a lot of kids. Now kids have a lot of parents.

With divorce and remarriage so common, stepfamilies are the growth industry of the new millennium. Children often must learn to live with new parents and new siblings, which isn't easy.

Blending families sounds like such a great idea, until you do it. "I've got kids who need a dad, you've got kids who need a mom, let's throw our beans together in the same pot." It seems to make a lot of sense. But when you get into the nitty-gritty of building a new home out of two different families, sparks will fly. You may actually long for the simplicity of single parenting.

After I spoke recently at a seminar in Minnesota, a couple came up and said, "We just wanted to tell you how much your book *Living in a Stepfamily without Getting Stepped On* has meant to us." And I in my deep humility expected to hear from these stepparents how my brilliant insights had made their lives wonderful and peaceful. Instead, they surprised me with their frankness.

"Your book prepared us for the 'Armageddon evenings' we've been experiencing," they said. "Living in a stepfamily is tremendously difficult. Thanks for letting us know that." Their comments were sobering, but right on target. Even if you do everything right, a blended family is still a war zone.

I often say that, at a wedding, more than two people are getting married. Try six. You have to count both sets of parents too. In a very real sense, you are "marrying" your in-laws. Like it or not, you marry *into* a family.

But what if the bride and the groom each have children? The same principle applies, but the numbers increase exponentially. You're "marrying" your spouse's mom and dad and son and daughter, and your spouse is marrying yours. Your children are suddenly gaining new brothers and sisters *and grandparents*. There may be twenty or thirty "marriages" going on in that one ceremony!

The point is that blending families is complicated. You must enter that situation with your eyes wide open. If you expect this marriage to solve all your single-parenting problems, forget it. You're just opening a new can of concerns.

When only one of the partners has children, it's a bit simpler, but there are still blending issues. The new father or mother has to earn the right to be a parent, and that may take some time.

In general, it takes three to seven years for families to blend. Three to seven years! That means your sixth-grader may be out of the house by the time you start to feel like a single family. It's a long haul. Along the way, reality discipline will help you, but be careful how you apply it. The following guidelines should help.

Discipline Your Own Kids at First

Remember that "relationships come before rules," and you don't have much of a relationship yet with your spouse's children. Thus it will be hard for you to lay down the law. And if you ever need to "pull the rug out," your stepkids will only resent it. Each parent should discipline only his or her own children for the first few years. Eventually the family will gel enough so that's not necessary.

This may create some imbalance if one parent is harsher than the other. The parents should work together to apply reality discipline in a consistent way, "comparing rulebooks" (see below). But a little imbalance is better than the resentment caused by inappropriate discipline from a stepparent.

Create a New Home

I'm not being metaphorical here. Literally move into a new house or apartment as you merge your families. When one family moves into the other's home, one will feel alienated and the other will feel crowded. It's much better to start a new living adventure for the whole group. I recognize that finding a different place to live is a big deal, but it's one of the many things you need to consider before you blend your families. If you've already moved your blended family into his or her home, you're probably already seeing the difficulties. The "host" family resents sharing "their" bedrooms, bathrooms, TVs, computers, and phones. The "guest" family never really feels at home. Try to remedy this as soon as possible by finding a home that's new for all of you.

Compare Rulebooks

I counsel all couples to do this, whether they have children or not. Recognize that you each grew up with a different set of expectations. What's right, what's wrong.

What's courteous, what's selfish. What the mommy does, what the daddy does. Your "rulebook" was given to you by your parents, though you may have edited it as you grew up. And in your previous marriage more adaptations occurred. Your children learned certain rules and expectations. But your spouse grew up with different rules and expectations and adapted them along the way, so that his or her kids have a completely different rulebook than your kids do.

What can you do? Talk about it, and keep talking about it. Get the whole family's input on the rights and wrongs of family life. Draw up a common set of expectations and responsibilities.

And as a stepparent, maintain a certain humility. You *don't* know what makes your stepkids tick. You may think they're sassing you when they're just being playful. You may disapprove of things they've been allowed to do all their lives. The old "I-language" comes in handy here. You can express your disapproval ("I don't like it when you do that"), but don't assume you know their intentions ("You're so rebellious!").

They Don't Have to Love You, Just Respect You—and Vice Versa

There are some all-out wars that erupt between stepparents and stepchildren. Your spouse's children have a lot of reasons to hate you, though most of these are irrational. They might consider you an imposter, stepping into the role of their real parent and not measuring up. They might blame you for preventing their parents from getting back together. They might resent you for "stealing" their mother or father (your spouse) away from them; they used to get that parent's full attention and now they share it with you. Or they might have impossibly high expectations of you and then be disappointed when you fail to meet them.

You can try to prove yourself, talk them out of those feelings, or say you love them, but you probably won't change much. If they're still nursing a lot of hurt, they'll pin it on you. And the more you try to force them to love you, the less they will. Love can't be forced.

But you can ask for respect. As you enter this stepparenting relationship, understand what kind of relationship it is and don't try to make it more than it is. (That would only increase their resentment.) In time, you may win the love of your stepkids, but it may take a lot of persistence on your part. In the meantime, you are in a position of quasi-authority over them. Yes, their own parent will be managing their discipline, but you are joining in the management of the home, and so they need to show you respect as the co-manager of the home and as the person their parent loves.

And it's well within the bounds of reality discipline to demand respect. If those kids visited a stranger's home and showed blatant disrespect, they'd be shown the door. That's reality. You and your spouse should agree on certain standards of respect your stepchildren should show you, along with appropriate disciplinary measures.

But the best way to win respect is to *give it*. Sometimes stepparents confess to me that they really don't love their spouse's children. Fine, I say. You don't have to love them, just respect them. At the very least they are human beings who live in your home. They are also the offspring of the one you love. They have feelings and ideas and dreams and goals. The more you listen to them, the more you treat them with honor and respect, the safer they will feel with you. Eventually they will return that respect.

I know it feels like a war zone sometimes. We get so embattled that we treat these stepfamily members worse than we would treat strangers in our home. Stop fighting and start showing common courtesy again. Don't bemoan the lack of love in that relationship. Strive for a respectful coexistence and the love will come.

Consider the Birth Order Blender

I've long been fascinated by the way our birth order affects our personalities. First-born, middle-born, and last-born children have distinctive traits, and once you learn what these are, you recognize them everywhere you go. Once, being interviewed about *The New Birth Order Book,* I surprised the four hosts of the ABC-TV talk show "The View" by correctly guessing the birth-order position of each of them. (Meredith Vieira was especially impressed when I accurately guessed that she had older *brothers.*)

But this is more than a parlor game. It's crucial information for you as you put together new relationships. I counsel pre-marital couples to consider how their birth order will express itself in their marriage. Some combinations fit nicely; others are more explosive. The same thing is true when blending families, only you have more combinations to consider.

First borns tend to be the most responsible; they grow up fastest. Often they're ambitious and perfectionistic. Last borns tend to be outgoing, attention-seeking. They're the "baby" of the family and they carry that designation throughout their lives. Middle-born children often get lost in the shuffle. They have to work harder to carve out a niche. So, while they're often peacemakers, mediating their siblings' disputes, they also become outsiders, mysterious, hard to know. An only child seems to exhibit the traits of a first born in triplicate, while some others curiously mix the traits of the adultlike first born with those of the attention-seeking last born.

Certainly there are exceptions to these tendencies, and various factors in a family may change the roles of different children, but the pattern is widespread. I discuss all this in detail in *The New Birth Order Book.* The point here is that a blended family usually jumbles everything up. The first born

159

in one family may suddenly acquire two older siblings. The baby of one family may have to share the spotlight with a new baby. This can cause frustration and acting out—even if the children don't understand their own feelings. It's as if they're actors on a stage but you've suddenly switched the roles around. They don't know which role to play, and that makes them very anxious.

It's very important for the new family to have a unique place for everyone. If you recognize the birth-order roles each child has played, you can give them appropriate support. The former first born who now has older siblings can continue to take on responsibility. Don't overlook his leadership role. And be sure to keep paying attention to your former youngest child, even if there's now a younger one in the home. Middle borns usually have less of an adjustment to make (they're still in the middle) and you can use their peacemaking abilities to calm conflicts among the others.

Allow Them to Grieve for the Lost Past

Stepfamilies are born out of loss. Death or divorce has ripped the old family apart, and here's a new arrangement that seems to replace the old one. Children will have a lot of conflicting feelings about that. On the one hand, they've harbored the hope that the pain of the past would be undone. Here's a chance to patch everything back together—a new home, just like the old one—or so they hope. But they quickly realize that it's not like the old one. They start comparing every new thing to their memories of the old thing, and the new thing comes up short.

"Stepdad doesn't let me do stuff like Dad used to."

"I liked it better when I had a room all to myself."

As your children realize that the new is no substitute for the old, they may get mad at you, the parent, for trying to dupe them. "If you're trying to make everything all better, it's not working." They may fight to preserve the memory of *the way it was*, and they may fight *you* because they think you're trying to erase that memory.

When people suffer loss, it's natural to grieve. The classic stages of grief are denial, anger, bargaining, depression, and finally acceptance. (There's a general progression through those stages, but a lot of bouncing around.) You need to let your kids go through that. In the process, they might withdraw and pretend everything is the way it was, scream at you for every little thing, try to wreck your new marriage so you can remarry your old spouse, or refuse to participate in any family activities.

As the parent, you must keep communicating the reality of the situation. The past is gone but not forgotten. You all feel bad about losing the old family, but you can't stay chained to the past. The new arrangement is not a substitute for the old one, but a whole new adventure. We need you to participate in this new family now, because that's the reality we face at this moment.

Deal with Anger

The foundation of the blended family is cemented with the mortar of anger, guilt, jealousy, anger, love, mistrust, anger, anxiety . . . and did I mention anger? As I just described, anger is one stage of the process of grieving our losses. But anger also runs rampant in a home where kids are struggling with other kids to find their place. There will also be anger at the new stepparent in any attempt to set new rules for the family. Everybody has an axe to grind.

People get angry when they think they're being treated unfairly. And a blended family creates so many new decisions, parceling out responsibilities, allowances, space in

161

the house, time with the TV or phone, attention of the parents, etc., that even Solomon would be befuddled. Everybody will feel they're getting the short end of something, not to mention the unfairness of being in a broken family to begin with. Your kids have a chip on their shoulder the size of Cleveland.

I recommend that blended families have a weekly anger meeting. Give each person a chance to say what's making them mad. These meetings can be explosive, so you'll need to establish some ground rules, but it's important to give your kids a chance to vent. If they bottle up that anger, it will come out in unhealthy ways.

Avoid Triangles of All Sorts

In chapter 8, I cautioned single parents about getting in the middle of your child's relationship with your ex. Such triangles are always unhealthy. In blended families, there are many more triangles to avoid. There's your ex and your partner's ex, and your kids and your partner's kids—you do the geometry.

It's common for children to fight a stepparent for "control" of their parent. Again and again, I've heard about stepchildren's efforts to sabotage the new marriage. Say the couple plans a weekend off by themselves; a kid will fake an illness just to keep them from going. There are regular attempts to pose the question, "Who's more important: me or your spouse?"

You can fight and win these battles, but I think it's wiser to step out of the triangle. That is, find visible ways to support your spouse's relationship with his or her children. As the children realize it's not an either-or situation, they'll have less to fight about.

Children may also make efforts to pit you against their "real" mom or dad. You may find this hurtful, but don't get drawn into a struggle. This is not a competition. And children will continue to play matchmaker between you and your ex. This is another triangle to avoid.

Often you will need to step in and resolve disputes among your children and stepchildren, but whenever possible try to get them to resolve things on their own. When you get in the middle, you'll be seen as siding with one or the other. It's good reality discipline to ask them to work out their own conflicts.

Prize Individuality but Expect Contribution

In any family, all members ought to be uniquely treated and treasured. Listen to the ideas and dreams of each one, feed their interests, and celebrate their talents. This is especially important in a blended family, where children can quickly feel lost and unappreciated.

But one of the best things you can do to make a child feel important is to give him or her a chance to contribute to the family. Give each child a responsibility to fulfill, perhaps some job around the house. As you assign these roles, take each child's age, ability, and interests into account. In fact, it's a good idea to talk about these roles at a family meeting, allowing children to choose their own responsibilities. They'll contribute more cheerfully if they've had some input. But then insist that they carry out their responsibilities or face discipline.

Prepare for Grenades Your Ex Will Toss

Ex-spouses have a way of making life miserable. Not all of them. I've seen a number of amicable divorces. But your

163

ex has the ability to mess things up for you in a big way, chiefly by stirring up the children.

Your ex might disappoint them, spoil them, make impossible promises to them, teach them bad habits, or turn them against you. If you share legal custody in any way, you have to send your kids off with this person and then deal with the fallout later.

I don't have any easy answers for you here. Just know that this might happen, and be as honest as you can with your kids about it. Don't poison their relationship with your ex, but try to help them see reality. Try not to get emotionally wrapped up in a conflict with your ex. Your ex-spouse probably knows how to push your buttons. But steel yourself to those shenanigans and focus on your new relationship and your new family. Do your best to prepare your kids and stepkids for life in the real world.

Establish the Strength of Your Marriage as the Centerpiece of the Family

In a blended family, the husband and wife must blend first. If that relationship is strong, the rest will follow.

It's an interesting question: "Who's more important to you: your spouse or your kids?" Sure, you love them all, but who's most important? In a first marriage, there's usually no problem saying the spouse has preeminence. After all, that relationship came first.

So when I say that a strong marital relationship must come first, serving as the centerpiece for a strong family, that only makes sense. But it's trickier in a blended family. Here the relationships with your children have seniority. Your spouse is relatively new. How can this new romance be more important than the children who bear your blood?

Still, for your family to have any kind of stability, it must be that way. Your relationship with your spouse must be a firm anchor. Your kids will test it, fight it, and resent it. If you don't make it clear from the start that your spouse comes first, your kids might just succeed in pulling your marriage apart.

But it's not an either-or situation, even though your children might press that point. Your marriage does not demote your kids to a lower status. You don't love them less because you have a new person to love (and a new family to love). Take every opportunity to communicate your enduring love to your kids, but also let them know how much you love your spouse.

Build a Team

The success of your blended family depends on the whole crew pulling together. You cannot demand allegiance; you have to earn it. So don't force things, especially at the start. Be respectful. Listen to the children. You don't have all the answers—let them know that. Don't make decisions that affect others in the family without checking with them. Build a team.

It will take three to seven years for your family to blend. You can hasten that process by honoring each person as a valued team member.

✔ To Review and Apply

Why is it important to "create a new home" for your blended family? Besides actually moving to a new place (which is recommended), how else can you do this?

165

What have been your biggest challenges as a blended family?

Which of the suggestions in this chapter seem hardest for you to follow? Which seems easiest? Why?

✔ To Practice

Make a plan to put into practice the hardest suggestion you just mentioned and the easiest. Be specific about meetings, conversations, policies, people, etc.

PART 2

Using Reality Discipline in the Everyday Hassles

Ten

How to Act When They Act Up

A few years ago, you'd see kids fussing with Tamagotchi pets. These virtual critters were actually tiny computers that required certain care in order to act properly. Their owners had to push certain buttons to feed them, walk them, even pet them. If they didn't get the proper treatment, they'd misbehave . . . and eventually just stop. These gadgets were all the rage for a while there. Kids were stopping in the middle of their classes, dates, and TV-viewing to push the right buttons to keep these little contraptions happy. And I'm sure that many of them would still complain and procrastinate when asked to feed their *real* pets.

Sometimes I think parents wish their kids were more like those tiny computers. Often I get questions from parents who want to "push the right buttons." They put me in the role of "answer man," and they assume that their problems will go away if they just follow my instructions perfectly.

I'm sorry if this is disappointing to you, but whatever "answers" I provide in this book are *not* guaranteed prescriptions for perfect parenting. As I've worked with thousands of families over the years, I've learned that what works with one child may not necessarily be the answer for another.

Having said that, let me reiterate my belief that reality discipline does work. Its principles are solid. Yet the way you use it may vary, and some ways may be better than others. Reality discipline is more of an art than a science. It's not button-pushing, but it does get results when used sensitively and creatively, with an awareness of your child's uniqueness.

In these last three chapters, I offer suggestions for coping with common scenarios in the home. How do you apply reality discipline in these cases? This chapter concerns certain behaviors of your children. What should you do when they do this? The following chapters cover specific family situations and then parental strategies. Within each chapter, the subjects are arranged alphabetically. I'm hoping you can use this as a resource you can use repeatedly as your children grow.

Attention Seeking

The parent using reality discipline understands that children are always going to seek attention. From our earliest moments in life, we all seek attention in some shape or form. Infants, for example, learn they can get attention through crying. If the parents are always there to pick up the child at first peep, the child learns that as small as he might be he has a great deal of power and influence over adults.

As children grow, they begin to seek attention in positive ways. If they don't get attention and recognition through positive means, they turn to a myriad of negative methods that range from whining to dawdling behind, from tapping a pencil on the desk to combing hair at the dinner table.

Very early in life, children can develop faulty beliefs about themselves and others that, if not checked, will continue into adulthood. Examples of faulty thinking in a child's mind include: *I only count in life when I'm noticed. I only count in life when I can control or dominate or win.*

I say these are faulty ideas because they are simply not true. We do not count in life only when we can get the attention of others. As those who have been created by God, we already count. What we must do is meet our Maker on his ground and come to an understanding of his plan for us while we live on this earth.

The child's natural desire for attention is a critical reason parents must take the time to train their children. We must take the time to enter each child's private world. We must get behind his or her eyes and see life as our son or daughter sees it.

As for how to get behind the eyes of your child, I suggest that you do a little "psychological guessing." Sit down with your child, look him right in the eye, and say, "You know, honey, I could be wrong, but as I watch you and your brother fighting, I get the idea you don't really hate your brother that much. It's just that you want a little more attention from me—that somehow you want to know that I really love and care about you. Is that what's really going on?"

Fears

Children—particularly the very young, under six years of age—frequently have fears. Fears come in all sizes and shapes: nightmares, fears of the dark, and others. Most parents find that their children's fears center around nighttime, going to sleep, and being in the bedroom alone.

There are some very obvious ways to help your child conquer fears: night-lights and leaving the hall light on among

171

them. Every parent should be aware that *most* fears resulting in nightmares, night terrors, and abnormal thoughts and feelings are a direct result of allowing children to watch violence on television. Parents must be acutely aware of the potential long-term damage that can result from allowing their children to watch violent or frightening programs and films. Doctor James Dobson cites a study at Cornell University that demonstrated that middle-class fathers of pre-school children spent an average of thirty-seven seconds a day with their children—that's less than five minutes a week! In contrast, it showed that children watched television fifty-four hours per week!

One of the best ways to help your children with their fears is to talk about your own fears. Most of us, as children, had fears of one thing or another. It's good to share your own experiences with your child. Tell how you recognized and handled certain fears in your own life. Never criticize or reprimand your child for having fears. Whatever you do, don't make fun of him, no matter how amusing a certain remark he made might be. Help your child understand that everyone has fears and that with help and encouragement, he can overcome what is making him afraid.

Keep in mind, however, that a child may use fear in the same way he might use remorse—as a ploy or a manipulative tool. Children are masters at needlessly involving Mom and Dad in their lives. They want to monopolize their parents and will go to great lengths to do so. At a very young age, they can become masters at this art.

One of the suggestions I make to parents of young children (under five) is that bedtime itself should include a built-in routine. As the child gets tucked in there can be a prayer time plus a story time, or perhaps you may want to play a recording. Make it clear that there is one story or one playing of a record and then the door is closed and it is not to open again. (See the section on "Bedtime Battles" in the next chapter.)

Fighting

Many parents I talk to seem to believe it's impossible to have children who don't fight. Yet I also know of families in which fighting among siblings is minimal. If we understand the dynamics of why children fight, we can make some inroads in correcting the situation.

Realize first of all that when two of your children fight, they are cooperating with each other. It seems odd to call fighting an act of cooperation, but that is exactly what is happening. It is extremely difficult to get a fight going with only one person. As the old cliché puts it, "It takes two to tango." The other person has to say just the right word, or use just the right facial expression or gesture, to get the fight going and to keep it going.

I have found that the best way to handle fighting is to give the children what they seem to say they want. If they want to fight, let them fight. I always tell parents, however, that they have the right to say where the children can fight and under what conditions. If the children fight, it cannot interfere with the peace and welfare of others in the home.

When two children start fighting, it is best to guide them (if they're little, carry them) to a room elsewhere in the house, or possibly to the backyard. Give them instructions to continue fighting until they have worked out their problem. Leave them to their "fight." In most cases, when you give children permission to fight, they won't. They merely stand and look at each other. One might say, "All right, you start it." And the other one replies, "No, *you* start it."

What usually happens is that neither of them starts it because they don't want to fight that badly. Their fighting, for the most part, was designed to get the parents needlessly involved in their hassles. The sooner parents learn to stay out of their children's hassles the sooner they will teach their children greater responsibility and accountability.

Many schoolteachers tell me that when they find children fighting they solve the problem this way: They give both children boxing gloves, take away their audience, put them in a gym, and tell them to go ahead and box it out. But in these situations the children seldom fight either. Children usually fight for attention. They want an audience—their peers or, if they are at home, their parents. Take away the audience and the fight usually stops.

There are, of course, exceptions to every rule or general principle. There are times when one child may pick a fight with another who is totally outmatched in size and strength. I know of one mother who found her twelve-year-old choking his nine-year-old brother, who was rapidly turning blue. That was the day the boys got separate bedrooms!

Many times the fighting is not physical but verbal. There is a lot of bantering back and forth. Then it turns into name-calling and finally into a shouting match. If this happens at the dinner table, just excuse the children and tell them to leave the table and go to another part of the house or outside. If they are more interested in name-calling and arguing than they are in eating, they may do it elsewhere. It is usually a good idea to escort them to wherever you want them to go and then give them instructions to stay in the room or outside in the yard until they've worked out their problems. Only when they have worked out their problems and are willing to behave quietly may they rejoin the others at the dinner table.

Always be sure to let reality be the teacher. If dinner is over by the time the children get back, there will be no more food and no special meal for them. They will have missed their meal in order to engage in their fight. Reality has moved in to stress the need for social order and treating one another respectfully. If they can't get their disagreement settled before dinner is over, dinner is over anyway. It's a little like not getting your act together in the morning and running to catch the bus, only to see it pull away just as you round the corner.

Reality discipline stresses the realities in this world, and the realities say that certain things are done during a time frame. If you don't make one time frame, you have to wait for the next one. If you miss one bus, you must wait for the next one. If you miss one meal, you wait for the next one.

Fighting—verbal or physical—often occurs while the family is traveling in the car. In cases like this, it's best to pull over and stop. If possible, get out of the car and go for a short walk and allow the children to continue fighting. (They will soon stop.) If it is not safe to leave the car, simply tell the children that they can continue fighting but the car will not move until they are through.

The key here is to be calm and not get angry yourself. If the children are on the way to participate in one of their own activities (Little League baseball or football, music lesson, and so on), it will be all the better. There will be a natural consequence for their misbehavior.

I believe parents are being responsible when they decide not to operate a motor vehicle while a fight is in progress. Again, the message to the children is, "Well, you can fight, but I'm not going to continue until the fighting has stopped." The fighting usually stops in a minute or less. If the fighting does not stop, simply have the courage to turn around and drive back home.

In every case, your goal is to not encourage fighting. You want your children to see that fighting is not a good way to solve problems. You want your children to learn:

1. Fighting gets no payoff from Mom and Dad, not even a negative one.
2. If I fight, I can get hurt.
3. If I fight, I may not go to Little League, the park, or other places.

Remember, there is no way to eliminate rivalry between siblings. All you can hope for realistically is to minimize it. Conflict in the home, particularly among siblings, is natural. As you help your child learn to solve his conflicts in a positive way, you build his psychological muscles for dealing with the realities of life.

Forgetting

Does your child seem to suffer temporary losses of memory from time to time? I'm not talking about amnesia. I'm talking about those times when you ask him to do a particular task and later he responds by saying half apologetically, "Oh, I forgot."

What's important here is to realize *why* your child keeps forgetting things—particularly things you've asked him to do. Is the child getting a payoff from the forgetting? I'm not talking about an extra allowance. I'm talking about letting the child get away with another kind of manipulative ploy.

If you ask the child to do something and he forgets and then you go ahead and do the task for him, he is getting the payoff he is looking for. You have reinforced his forgetting habit and at the same time you have weakened the child in some serious ways. For one, you weaken his self-confidence. You also weaken his ability to think and to remember things that are important. In the long run, you weaken his ability to be accountable and responsible.

Whenever parents complain to me about their child's "forgetfulness," I immediately urge them to not let forgetting be an excuse for not doing a task. Reality discipline accepts no excuses. (You may accept reasons in extenuating circumstances but not continual excuses that fall into patterns.) Even if it's difficult and you feel like you are being "mean," remember that in the future your child will be working for people who will not accept excuses or apologies because he "forgot."

So, always stand on the basic principle. If your child's been asked to do something and then "forgets," make him do it anyway. If it means missing his favorite TV program, being late for where he is going (including school), or having to be inconvenienced in any number of other ways, so be it. Life will not tolerate your child's excuses and neither should you.

Lying

The parents I know want their children to tell them the truth. Parents are particularly concerned about lying and why their children sometimes resort to this kind of dishonesty. Lying usually falls into two basic patterns:

1. *Some children lie out of wish fulfillment.* This kind of lie expresses a simple childlike fantasy. Very young children sometimes fantasize about imaginary friends, seeing Rudolf the Red-Nosed Reindeer, and so on. These "lies" are usually isolated incidents and not something to be greatly concerned about.

2. *The reason most lies are told, however, is out of fear.* No matter how much a child is loved and accepted, he is afraid that if he tells his parents the truth about some misbehavior, something unpleasant will happen. He will be punished in some way. At the very foundation of his fears is the fear that if he tells the truth he will not be loved. The child sees himself as having to be perfect in order to deserve love.

Fibs or little white lies are often spontaneous attempts to cover up small imperfections. If a parent is authoritarian, it will set the stage for more lying. The child of the authoritarian parent is often defeated by unrealistic expectations (not to mention fear). Something else you can do is share your own imperfections with your child. Help him or her realize that all of us are imperfect in one way or another. Once, when my daughter Krissy was nine, she came to me in tears because she realized she had lied regarding a telephone call for me. Actually it was my fault. Without thinking I had told her to tell someone I wasn't home when in fact I was shaving in the bathroom.

Mothers sometimes tell their children they don't have time to bake cookies or make lemonade. In reality they have time but they don't have the energy. It is better to be honest and say, "I'm too tired," or even, "I'm not in the mood right now."

Most parents I deal with know something about having their children lie or at least shade the truth (white lies). In many cases, parents would settle for having the child tell the truth and that would be the end of it. There would be no punishment or any particular form of discipline. Unfortunately, there are times when the child has to be held accountable for lies and some kind of consequence has to be invoked. When this does happen, be sure to make it clear to the child that while he has lied and you have to invoke a consequence, you still love him very much and you hope he will not feel he has to lie in the future.

Parents can encourage their children to stop lying with the following strategies:

1. *Always trust your child.* Give him the opportunity to tell the truth. When he does tell the truth, thank him and try to go on from there. If a consequence is necessary, carefully explain why, but point out that the truth is always better than the lie.

2. *Always seize every opportunity to show children why lying never pays.* One lie always has to lead to another. I always like to tell my children, "If you don't lie, you don't have to have such a good memory." The liar is always having to remember what he said to whom, and when, and how he can cover up his last lie with another one.

Not Eating

We've already touched on this in earlier chapters. My work with parents and children tells me there are far too many hassles in the American home every night at the dinner table. It also happens at breakfast and lunch, but dinner seems to be the special time when little Rufus and little Jessica decide they are not going to eat.

My basic premise is that when a child doesn't want to eat, bribing and rewarding aren't going to work. Neither does "playing airplane," which went out twenty years ago. (In case you don't know how to play airplane, you say, "Open the hangar door," and on and on.)

Reality discipline has a simple approach to dealing with the child who does not eat. You simply hold him accountable for his choice. Remove the food from the plate, dump it in the garbage, and excuse the child from the table. This works with ten-year-olds as well as three year olds.

Actually, removing the food and excusing the child is the easy part. The hard part comes when you have to back up your actions by refusing the child any more food for the evening. Here is where you have to let the child experience the reality of being hungry because he chose not to eat dinner. If you call little Rufus's bluff, take away his food, and tell him, "Dinner is over for you. Run along and play," you can be sure that a couple of things will soon happen:

1. *Rufus will be back shortly, whining and fussing that he is hungry.* At this time you simply say, "I'll bet you are. Could it have anything to do with the fact that you didn't eat your dinner, Snookums?"

2. *The other thing that is very likely to happen is that the child will eat a huge breakfast the next morning.* I know some of you are probably thinking, *What? Let my child miss a meal?* Your pediatrician will tell you that a child will not die if he misses

179

a meal—and that missed meal will do much to teach your child what reality is all about.

When your child wants to play the "I'm not hungry" game, it's important that you don't fall into the same old trap that some of our parents did when we were kids. No bribing, rewarding, cajoling, pleading, threatening, screaming, or spanking. Give the child the right to make his own decision and then hold him accountable.

Oh, yes, if it goes too hard against your grain to dump the food in the garbage, simply put it in the refrigerator for leftovers.

Selfishness

A definite reality of life is that our children are self-centered little creatures. Many times we are left shaking our heads, wondering why our kids can only think of themselves. The answer is simple. They are children and it is characteristic of a child to think only of himself. He has to learn how to think of others.

It is ironic that while one of the chief responsibilities of parents is to help their children learn how to think of others and not only of themselves, at the same time a key error that many parents make is to focus on pleasing their children and making them happy. I'm not saying that we should try to make our children miserable. But I see case after case where parents are so busy making their children happy and trying to do what pleases them that any teaching they are trying to do about "thinking of others instead of yourself" is lost in the shuffle.

One typical example of how this happens is in the category of giving your children gifts. I do a lot of traveling and I am sympathetic toward parents who want to bring home gifts from their travels to give to the children. I have done it myself. But I also try to caution parents (myself included) to not *always* bring a treat home for a child. If this becomes a regular routine, the child views the gift as his right. People don't have a "right" to a gift. A gift is supposed to be an act of affection toward another person.

I recall a TV talk show interview. The host asked me what I thought he should do about his son. It seems that his nine-year-old often did not like the gifts the talk show host brought home from his travels. His boy was energetic, affectionate, and by all standards a "pretty good kid." But he soon turned his "dislike" for his father's gifts into a sort of game. Almost every time his father brought him a gift, he would carry on and complain. The father ended up feeling guilty and irritated because he had knocked himself out to bring home an appropriate gift, and the boy didn't like it.

I told the talk show host that the next time this happened he should proceed as follows: As soon as the boy expressed dislike or disdain for a gift, the father should simply say, "I'm sorry you don't like it. May I have it back, please? I'm sure you don't want to be bothered with it."

Then the father could take it and do one of several things. Perhaps a younger or older brother or sister might like the gift. Or perhaps a neighbor child would appreciate the gift. Whatever was done should be done swiftly and directly. If possible, the gift could even be returned where it was purchased.

I cautioned the father to do all this calmly and with love. If the child sensed that the father was simply "getting revenge" or was simply venting hurt feelings, the discipline would be ineffective. What the father was trying to do, in this case, was simply communicate to his son, "Hey, I love you. I bring you gifts because I want to tell you how much I love you. If you don't like the gifts, then I don't imagine you want them cluttering up your room."

I made one other suggestion to the talk show host father. It is something I try to do myself. Parents should get out of the habit of bringing home gifts every time they travel. If a

181

parent has to travel a great deal, he may use gifts as a bribe or a way of relieving his own guilt. But gifts should be a treat given once in a while, not every week, every month, or every trip. What we really want to teach children is that they should be happy that Daddy is back home. They should experience the joy of Daddy's homecoming and not necessarily the joy of receiving another gift.

Another means of combating self-centeredness in children is to start teaching them at an early age that it is truly more blessed to give than to receive. They should be encouraged to do things for other people whenever possible. For example, there might be an elderly couple in the neighborhood who could use some chores done, free of charge. If you really want to make this effective, make it a family project. Mom, Dad, and the kids can all go over and do some yard work for such a couple as an act of love. *Showing* your kids how to be unselfish is far more effective than *telling* them.

Sexual Exploration

Whenever I am speaking at a seminar and the topic of sex comes up, the crowd becomes notably more quiet. I think the reason for this is that, particularly in America, we have never become comfortable with speaking about sex. When I talk with mothers and fathers in my office, they often report that their children have discovered their genitalia and are "touching themselves," and what should they do?

My first piece of advice is to not panic. Children do, in fact, discover their genitalia almost immediately after birth and they continue to have a fascination with touching themselves.

But how are the parents supposed to talk to a child when this occurs? I believe the key is to convey to the child that it's very natural to want to touch your own body. At a very early age, give him or her guidelines that it's okay to touch yourself, but that you should not touch other people's bodies without their permission.

Of course, there are situations where other children do "give their permission." Kids are well known for playing house or doctor and "checking each other out." How is a parent to handle this? First of all, understand that the motivation for "playing doctor" usually stems from a child's need to determine if all boys and girls are built the same. About 95 percent of the men and women I work with in private practice admit to sexual exploration (playing doctor) with same-sex children when they were small.

If you do find your child or children playing doctor, the more calmly you react to such normal behavior, the better. Simply take your child aside and explain that his or her curiosity is very natural. However, caution your child that touching the bodies of others can create upsetting feelings. Tell your child you will talk with him or her about bodies and how they function. Tell him that you'll get a book that will "help us answer the questions we have."

I also recommend telling the other child or children's parents involved in the playing-doctor episode about the "clinic" you conducted with your own child, and briefly outline the course of action you plan to take.

And then follow through with what you said you would do. Get an appropriate book (a good one is *The Wonderful Story of How You Were Born* by Sidonie Gruenberg, published by Doubleday). Use the book as a springboard to further discussions.

I also highly recommend to parents that they share with their children about times they played doctor when they were young. I recommend this because such an admission reinforces in the child's mind that what he has done is natural and not something to feel guilty about. It also opens many avenues for further communication. The principle of reality discipline is that the parents must be willing to share the realities of their own experiences with their children in order to have honest and open communication.

Never punish a child for natural curiosity about his or her body. If you are overreactive and produce guilt and fear in your child, you may sow seeds in his mind that will sprout into abnormal sexual attitudes later in life.

Playing doctor is one problem, but what does a mother do when she finds her five-year-old daughter stimulating herself while sitting on the floor watching Saturday-morning cartoons? The key to any encounter with your children over the touching of their genitals is to be calm, warm, and positive. Never be critical, condemning, or hysterical. You do not want your children to associate their genitalia with something bad, evil, or dirty.

In every way possible, try to convey to your children at an early age that all parts of their bodies are good, wonderful, and given by God. Everything we are is part of God's plan for our lives. As your children get older (above six) you can start talking about the gift of sex and how Mommy and Daddy make babies. I have already mentioned an excellent book by Sidonie Gruenberg. Another good one is *How to Teach Your Child about Sex* by Grace H. Ketterman, M.D. (Revell).

Seminar audiences often ask me to share any experiences that my wife and I have had in this area with our own children and their exploration of the genitalia. The most humorous incident occurred one day while I was at the office. The phone rang and it was Sande, who was practically hysterical. She was crying and all I could get out of her was that something was wrong with Kevin, who was nineteen months old at the time. I immediately thought of our swimming pool in the backyard and thought the worst. Had she discovered him floating in the pool? No, that wasn't it.

"Well, then, what's wrong?" I asked. "Tell me, quick."

"Well," she said, "well, it's his thing."

"His thing?"

"Yes—you know, his *thing.*"

"Well, what's wrong with his thing?" I asked.

"It's purple!" she burst out.

"It's purple?" I echoed. "What do you mean, it's purple?"

Sande went on from there to explain that little Kevin had taken down his diapers, found a purple Magic Marker, and had done some rather creative artwork on his "thing." Then he came marching out into the family room like Napoleon to show my wife.

At this point I broke up laughing. I shouldn't have laughed, but I couldn't help it.

"Well, why are you laughing?" Sande asked.

I could tell she wasn't too happy with my amusement.

"Well, honey," I replied. "Little boys do things like that— you shouldn't worry."

Sande was incredulous. "They *do?*" she said. "Do you think it's *really* okay?"

"At nineteen months, it's okay," I assured her. "I just hope he doesn't get a rash."

And so, that was the day my wife learned that little boys do many "funny little things like that." The point of the story is that children are going to experiment—with themselves and sometimes with one another. Reality discipline demands that you keep your cool and never communicate to the child that his honest curiosity is dirty or perverted. At the same time, always stress the private nature of the sexual organs and that God gave us our sex organs as part of his wonderful plan for our lives.

Swearing

One day my six-year-old suddenly turned the air blue with a four-letter word. Her mother looked at me and I looked at her. Then we both looked at our daughter. Without a word, I picked her up, took her to her bedroom, and sat her on the bed. My six-year-old was surprised by her quick removal to her room. Her eyes were like Ping-Pong balls. I

185

looked her right in those Ping-Pong-ball-sized eyes and said, "Krissy, Daddy and Mommy know every filthy and dirty word in the book. But we have the choice not to use those words."

Of course, Krissy was in tears by now and very sorry for what she had said. We assured her that we forgave her and then we made a point to talk with her about the fact that she was going to hear that kind of word in school and on the playground. She would see filthy words written on rest room walls and she was going to hear adults use them as well. This is the reality of the situation. As much as we hate to see it, our children are exposed to ugly, filthy, profane words early in their lives and it continues throughout life.

I believe that the key approach when you hear your child swearing or talking obscenely is to let the child know that you know all the words—every one of them—but you have chosen not to use them. Tell the child specifically why you have chosen not to use these words. If the words include taking God's name in vain, explain to your child that in your home you choose not to use that kind of language because it is crude, ignorant, and disrespectful for all concerned.

The above approach is infinitely better than traditional punitive measures such as a slap in the face, a spanking, or the classic "washing the child's mouth out with soap." All of these may relieve your tensions and anger, but they will have nothing to do with discipline or training.

Talking Back

Unless you are running your home with the authoritarian precision of a dictator, your children probably feel free to talk back to you on occasion. Many parents I deal with have a real problem when their children "smart mouth" them. They want their children to be able to challenge them and to say how they feel, but when they cross that unseen but very real line and become impudent, a little switch goes off inside a parent's brain. A little voice says, *You can't say that to me. Don't you know who I am? I'm your mother!*

Sometimes the parent feeds that exact message right back to the child and, of course, this can lead to more talking back and more impudence.

When your child becomes powerful with you, you should not become powerful in return. All you do by trying to exert your power is to lay the foundation for a good knock-down-drag-out battle. There are any number of ways to handle talking back.

If you have trouble keeping your temper, you might try leaving the room for a minute or two. This conveys to the child, "I choose not to fight with you." A short trip to your bedroom perhaps, and turning the radio on (to drown out the back talk if necessary) can allow you to stay in control of your emotions. A caution here, however, is to only be gone a couple of minutes. You do not want the child to get the idea that he can "drive Mommy out" any time he wants. And once you have gotten control, you must go back and deal with the situation.

One way to deal with smart talk is to simply send the child an "I" message that says you do not appreciate this kind of behavior and will not tolerate it. If he chooses to continue this kind of talk, he will be the one who is removed from the scene and isolated for a brief time if necessary.

If a child persists in talking back, he may be asking for a swat. If the child is seven years old or under, a swat may well be in order. Just be sure that you are in control of your emotions and that after the swat you let the child know he is loved but he cannot talk that way to his parents.

Suppose the "talking back" is centered around what little Jessica is going to have to wear to a birthday party. If Jessica gets very vocal and abusive in protesting what she has to wear, you can "pull the rug" by simply announcing, "I guess you are not going to the party."

Whatever parents do, I insist that they never accept smart-mouth behavior. Furthermore, it is essential for women not to take any guff from their sons as well as for dads to not take any guff from their daughters. There is a very powerful relationship between a mother and her son and a dad and his daughter. What parents are really doing is training their children to learn who they are as male and female and what being a man or woman is all about. It is particularly important for mothers not to train their sons to believe that they can walk all over women.

Psychological research continues to demonstrate that men tend to marry women who have personality traits similar to their mothers, and women tend to marry men with personalities similar to their fathers. This kind of research evidence only underlines the need for parents to be aware of the "specialness" of mother-son, father-daughter relationships. When parents stand their ground with opposite-sex children, they are actually teaching a great deal about respect and love in a marriage relationship. It may not be evident at the moment, but when Mom refuses to let little Buford get away with smart talk, and when Dad brings little Jessica up short for a fit of temper, they are actually increasing their children's chances for ultimate marital happiness in the future.

A key concept with which reality discipline agrees completely is: "God didn't create any of us to be walked on!"

Tattling

One of the oldest and most potent tricks children use to needlessly drag parents into their hassles is tattling on one another. The problem with allowing tattling to ever start is that once you hear one tale, you are going to have to listen to all of them. I suggest to parents that they never listen to anything that sounds like tattling. Of course, the parent must be able to differentiate between the kind of talebearing that is designed to simply get a brother or sister in trouble and a report of something of a more serious nature. For example, if a twelve-year-old brother is beating up on an eight-year-old sister, the sister should have some kind of recourse to let Mom know she is getting worked over. But in many cases, children will come with their little stories about what big brother is doing or about what sister did, and so on.

When you can detect that no real harm is being done, just make a direct statement such as, "Honey, I'm sure you can handle it. You and your sister work it out." Make this kind of encouraging statement, which tells your child that you are not going to give in and be used or manipulated. Again, let me emphasize that there are times when a child may have a bona fide complaint. But if you can detect that he or she is simply trying to manipulate you to get his own way, you must act quickly to put a stop to it. Otherwise, you walk directly into the trap. You will be running around in circles as each child yanks you on the end of his own little chain to get you involved.

When you allow the child to jerk you around like this, you inevitably have to play the old judge-and-jury game in which you have to make a decision based upon very limited and biased information which has been given to you by one or both of your children. Reality discipline does not work well when you have to play judge and jury. You want reality to be the teacher and the judge if judgment is necessary. Whenever possible, stay out of the hassles and disagreements that your children get into and let them be accountable for their own actions. When necessary you may have to step in, but these times should be kept to a minimum.

I know of one mother who tried to keep tattling in proper perspective this way: When any of her three children came with his tale of woe, she would listen carefully. If it was a simple "Brian hit me" or "Vicki won't let me play" tale, the mother would respond, "Thank you," and nothing was done. But if it was a genuine report of real abuse or mayhem that often involved two against one, with that one child in drastic trouble, then she would respond with appropriate action. Her children soon learned that when they just tattled they were usually ignored, and so they stopped giving those kinds of reports and just made the more genuine complaints.

Eleven

The Daily Battle

Parenting your children shouldn't be a battle, but you know it often is. In fact, sometimes it seems like an all-out war. Some kids discover that they have power, and so they use it. They test you again and again, in many of the situations you face daily. From waking up to bedding down, they're ready to pit their will against yours, and you've got to be ready.

Many parents learn to dread certain times of day, because they know little Sean or Sharisse is going to fight them. Whether it's "I don't want to get up yet," or "I won't eat that," or "Just ten more minutes before bedtime, okay?"—children are going to push the limits of your power over them. How will you respond?

The beauty of reality discipline is that it shifts the power struggle a bit. It's not just you against your kid. It's your kid against *reality*, and you're just there to guide the process. Sharisse may not want to get up in the morning, but if she's late to school there will be consequences. Sean may not want to eat his broccoli, but if he doesn't he'll be mighty hungry by morning. You're really not battling your children, you're fighting on their side as they face the harsh realities of life. Of course they may not see it that way.

This chapter focuses on those family situations in which you may encounter conflict. How can you apply reality discipline in those everyday moments?

Bedtime Battles

A classic problem occurs in many homes at bedtime. Children are often resistant to going to bed and/or hard to get settled down once they are in the sack.

A key to handling the "Can I stay up a little longer?" ploy is to use the standard rule of reality discipline: direct and swift action. Do not argue or negotiate. Announce: "Bedtime at eight o'clock," or whatever you have set. Then stick with it.

With younger children, you may have an established routine to read a story and say prayers. But when the routine is completed, tuck them in and close the door. It's time to sleep.

Now a powerful child will test you on that, screaming, whining, or carrying on in some other way. I have counseled parents whose children have screamed for four hours at a time. This can be extremely irritating and eventually the parent may weaken. But it doesn't do any good to hold out for an hour and forty-five minutes and then give in and go see what's wrong. All you teach the child then is to keep screaming; sooner or later Mommy or Daddy will give in.

If you are having trouble finding the right routine to get your child asleep, you might consider using a tape recorder with an automatic shutoff. Your local bookstore might have stories on tape that might lull your child to dreamland.

Whatever you try, remember these basic principles:

1. Create a routine the child can count on.
2. Use a recording as the last step in getting the child to sleep.

3. Once the child is tucked in, do not open the child's door for any reason.
4. If the child gets out of bed for any reason, he will have to tuck himself back in. Once he knows he won't get you to repeat the bedtime routine, he'll probably stay in bed.
5. Your tucking in and prayer time can be a wonderful opportunity to talk with your child about the events of the day (both your child's and yours). *Do not hurry while you are tucking your child in and praying with him.* This is your daily opportunity to communicate your love to your child at a critical moment. Do not rush off to catch a TV show. Your child is more important.

Older children (seven and above) will use all sorts of stalling tactics to avoid going to bed (especially if a certain TV show is about to start). They will haggle like used-car salesmen just to squeeze a few more minutes out of you. Don't play that game. Have a simple understanding: "Don't go to bed on time and your bedtime is even earlier for the next few nights." Or, "Don't go to bed on time and give up your favorite TV show for a week." The key is not to weaken or hesitate. Be pleasant and friendly, but imitate General Ulysses S. Grant. His motto was "unconditional surrender."

But suppose your little buzzards have gone quietly enough to their roosts for the night and after a few minutes you hear odd noises. (This is a typical problem when two children bunk together.) You can't concentrate on chatting with your spouse, on watching your program, or reading your paper. The thumps and squeals are just too loud. Once again the situation calls for action—direct and swift. What are your options?

You may or may not want to use a tactic I employed on one occasion. I recommend it as long as you use common sense and extreme caution. Our little girls, Holly and Krissy, were not settling down for the night. Before they knew it they were outside on the back porch in weather that was somewhat inclement (occasionally it does rain in Tucson). They stayed on the porch for exactly ninety seconds and then I let them back in. They went quietly to bed with no further delays or hassles.

If putting children outside for a brief time sounds too extreme or isn't practical, here are some other ideas: Take both children from their bedroom and put them in another room such as the kitchen, the sewing room, possibly even the bathroom. Give them instructions to sit there until they can work out their problem. Under no circumstances are they to have available a TV, a radio, or some other toy or device with which they can amuse themselves. The idea is to sit on separate chairs and have a period of "time out" while they settle down.

Another approach is to separate the children. If one of them is obviously the culprit in the hassle, take him and put him in another room for a brief time. Again, he is to sit on a chair and go through a time-out period of five or ten minutes, until he can go back to bed quietly.

A final option is a spanking, but chances are a swat will not be necessary. Once you take action, your children will be much more likely to settle down. Wrestling and giggling in bed together is fun. Sitting in a room together is not fun. You can work out your own best approach to using action and not words to fight the bedtime battle. There are any number of strategies for moving in with positive discipline without playing the games your kids want you to play: warnings, lectures, several trips to tell them to be quiet, and on and on.

Make clear to your children that bedtime is a must, not a negotiable option. They may protest, "But I'm not sleepy." Tell them, "Okay, you aren't sleepy, but it's still bedtime, so off to bed." Let them know that at the end of the day Mom and Dad need some moments by themselves to talk or do other things.

Courtesy

Another question I frequently get from mothers is, "How do I teach courtesy to my children? How can I teach them to say, 'Thank you,' 'You're welcome,' and 'Please'?"

Almost everyone I know—other counselors, therapists, teachers, and parents—agrees that teaching courtesy has to begin at a very early age, so that it becomes second nature to a child to be courteous. I advise parents to get together with their spouses and decide on just what they want to teach by way of courtesy. Do you want to teach your child to say, "Yes, sir," and, "No, ma'am"? The other common amenities are undoubtedly on the list: "Thank you," "Please," "You're welcome," "May I. . . ."

We all have our basic ideas on these, and we can keep trying to drum them into our children. But while correcting them and eliciting the proper response from them is certainly part of teaching courtesy, there is little question that the real way to teach courtesy is to be courteous yourself. As parents model courtesy—to one another as well as to their children—they will teach it.

One way we teach courtesy in our home is by playing a game at dinner that I call "The Penny Game." Everyone, adults included, gets five pennies. The object is to catch someone who isn't using proper table manners (chewing with mouth open, napkin not on lap, elbows on table, reaching in front of someone, being boisterous). As dinner progresses, everyone is watching everyone else to see if they can catch them and get one of their pennies. For example, if my daughter sees me doing something wrong and calls me on it, I have to give her a penny.

This is an excellent game for children ten years old and under. Our children always loved it. We've also had some good discussions that have come out of the game concerning why something is wrong and how it might be done better.

Suppose your child has said something discourteous to another person—child or adult. As I outlined in chapter 5, your best approach is to move in and "take the little buzzard by the beak." In other words, deal with the behavior then and there.

Do not reprimand your child in front of the offended party. Try to remove him from the room or at least go off a short distance and then speak to him. Gently but firmly tell him exactly what your feelings are about what he just said or did and why you feel that way. If the child is old enough (about three years or above), have him go back to the offended party and apologize. If the child refuses to do so, you may want to go to another form of discipline such as isolation: Remove him from the group for a set period of time.

What you should always seek, if at all possible, is to have the child say, "I'm sorry," "Please forgive me," "Excuse me"—something that will convey to the offended person or persons that the child is sorry.

I repeat, the best way to teach this kind of courtesy is to practice it yourself. If you ever offend your child or your spouse, be willing to say, "I'm sorry" without hesitation.

Courtesy is a good discussion topic for a family at dinner, or perhaps at special times such as just before going to bed. Talk with your children about showing courtesies of one kind or another to each other. (You may learn something about what your children see as a "common courtesy" toward them!) Come up with specific ideas for showing courtesy to others and, more importantly, help your child understand how it makes a person feel when someone is courteous or discourteous.

Dangers of Life

How does a parent go about talking to children about the realities of living in a world where dangers are always present?

One simple technique you can use as you drive along with younger children is to point out the squashed skunks, bashed bunnies, flat cats, demolished dogs, and dented deer to dramatize what happens when "we don't look both ways."

If you have a swimming pool, be aware that children from three to six years old will often tell you they can swim when they really can't. To a child, "swimming" can mean splashing around in a pool. Give neighborhood children a short swimming test *before* they can enjoy full use of your pool. Always advise older children about the depth of the pool. It is wise to restrict diving by children.

I also suggest—with a *strong* note of caution—to occasionally read newspaper accounts about drownings to your children, particularly an account that deals with someone just about their age. Do not overdo this because you can misuse the fear factor. What you are interested in is creating a healthy respect for the dangers involved with swimming pools.

One danger to children that has become more prominent in recent years is abduction by strangers. A number of TV specials have covered cases of missing children and how they were abducted. How can you teach your child about "stranger danger"?

This is also a sensitive area because you don't want to unduly frighten your children. On the other hand, you want your children to be aware. I believe the realistic approach is to simply tell the children honestly and quietly that everyone in the world is not like Mommy and Daddy. There are many nice people but there are some very bad people. Let your children know that everything in life that happens to people isn't necessarily good. If you aren't careful, some bad things can happen to you.

Parents can let their children know that God will protect them as they learn to use their heads and the brains that God gave them to think with.

Talk with your children and even go through little scenarios about what to do if a stranger comes up and offers a ride. Make it a firm rule in your family that your children never accept rides from strangers and, quite obviously, never hitchhike. (When I was assistant dean of students at the University of Arizona, too often coeds were raped as a result of hitchhiking.)

Help your child think of statements a stranger might make in order to get him or her into a car. Ploys that child abductors use include: "Your dog has been hurt and I can take you to him." "Your mommy [or daddy] has been in an accident and they sent me to come and get you."

Point out to your children that if Mommy or Daddy were hurt, it certainly wouldn't be a stranger who would come and pick them up.

Also, give them alternatives and plans of action if they ever are stopped by someone. Tell them not to argue with the person or to even talk with him. Tell them to politely decline the invitation and to move on quickly. If the person appears to make any kind of advance, the child should be ready to run for the nearest help—to a house where there is a light on or someone can be seen through the window, for example.

Many neighborhood schools have enlisted the help of parents to provide emergency assistance to children in case of an incident. A large *E* (or other symbol) is displayed in the front window of homes to signify that these parents have the authority and willingness to help a child in an emergency. Talk to your child about the problem, go over the child's route to school, and identify such homes so that the child knows in advance where he can find help.

I agree that it is a sad commentary that we have to warn our children about such things, but the statistics on children who are abused, used, kidnapped, and even killed are rising every year. This is reality and you should take the time to help them understand. You are not trying to frighten them but to make them wise. If your child is old enough to be away from you, even for the briefest amount of time, help him learn how to become responsible and able to make quick decisions that will help him avoid harm.

Dinnertime Strategy

I touch on mealtime problems such as not eating in many other places in this book, but here I want to suggest a basic strategy for helping you apply reality discipline at that critical hour called "dinnertime" when so many families seem to have a great deal of tension, stress, fighting, and upsets. Dinnertime should be one of the more fulfilling, comforting, and strengthening times of the day, but in too many homes it is precisely the opposite. What can be done?

First, commit yourself to breaking the typical routine that you've probably been using. This is especially true in homes where the children resist eating, gripe about the food, and so on. Have everyone sit down to dinner, but don't bother to put food on the plates of your children. Let the children ask for things to be passed. Let them take exactly what they want. Do not nag or coax them to eat their vegetables or be sure to drink their milk.

Do not coax or remind your children to finish their meal. Don't waste your breath with stories about people in the Far East who are starving to death. Your children know there is no way to send them any of the particular food the family has been served for that meal. Some children are even aware that in many Eastern countries the people are eating fish and other healthy foods and are in better shape than many overfed and underexercised Americans.

In general, treat your children as if they are adults who are accountable for how much food they take and how much food they eat.

Then sit back and listen. See if the conversation around the table changes. Talk about subjects of interest to you and to them. If they don't want to tell you what happened at school, don't worry about it. But do everything you can to maintain a casual, relaxed situation.

Be aware that your children will soon catch on to what you are trying to do and they will counterattack. They will lay traps and try to embroil you in controversy over whether they're eating or not eating. Just stay calm but firm. Don't get involved with what they are eating. Above all, enjoy your own meal.

For those parents who are both working, I add the following strategic suggestions. As I deal with families in which Mom has to work, I find that in many homes the children are expected to have dinner partially started, to have the table set, the garbage taken out, and so on. I believe children should be involved in doing chores in every home, but I especially applaud their involvement in the home where Mom and Dad are both working. When both parents have to work and Mom has little time to prepare dinner, assigning responsibilities to the children is a beautiful opportunity to put the principles of reality discipline to work.

But what if it doesn't seem to work? What if Mom and Dad come home and see that the table is not set, the garbage isn't out, and dinner is unstarted? The children are busy—off with their friends, repelling the latest Nintendo attack, and so on. What does reality discipline say at a moment like that? It says to use action, not words, but not the type of action you might think. Do not move in to invoke logical consequences. Do not do any reminding or coaxing, bribing or threatening, or blowing up. Simply sit down and read the paper. Relax and wind down from your busy day.

Sooner or later, one of your children will come in and ask the obvious questions: "When is dinner going to be ready? What's for dinner?"

Here is the opportunity for Mom or Dad to say in a low-key manner: "When the kitchen is ready for operation, dinner will be started. Right now, the kitchen looks as if no one is interested in dinner tonight. We can't prepare dinner in a messy, unsanitary kitchen."

This kind of response teaches your children that order is important. If they cannot help keep the house in an orderly condition, dinner will not be prepared.

Oh, yes, be sure you do not let your children "have dinner" by grabbing the nearest box of snack crackers or bag of chips and starting to munch away in front of the TV set. Let them know that no eating will be done until the responsibilities that were supposed to have been met are completed.

Getting Up in the Morning

From what I hear in counseling sessions and through questions I get in the mail, it would appear that many American homes are battle zones—especially in the morning. It seems to be a knock-down-drag-out battle to get little Buford out of bed and ready on time for school. Whenever mothers or dads approach me with the "How do I get my child to get up?" problem, I remind them of one of the basic principles of reality discipline: *You can't make another person do anything;* you guide him or her in such a way that reality makes him do what he needs to do.

So, the best way to proceed with the "can't get 'em up in the morning" crisis is to remove yourself from all responsibility. In other words, declare an armistice over the battle zone. You are not going to bug your child about getting up anymore.

Am I suggesting that you even allow the child to sleep in past the beginning of school hours? Absolutely. Let reality get your child up. After you have tried unsuccessfully a number of times to get your child up, simply refuse to cooperate. Refuse to be used as a human alarm clock. Tell your child he will have to figure out some way to get himself up. He will have to make some appropriate decisions about how he is going to get his body out of bed and off to school in the morning. If he fails to get to school, all kinds of reality will set in. The main reality will be big trouble with his teachers. True, the teachers may call you, but you simply will pass the message on to your child. Don't let the teachers intimidate you, put you on a guilt trip, or in some other way force you to go back to being a human alarm clock.

One obvious solution to the child's problem is that he get his own alarm clock. Provide him with one and show him how to set it. If he forgets to set his clock, he suffers the same kind of consequences that you do when you forget to set yours for an important date or meeting.

You may want to involve the child's teacher, or teachers, at school in your plan. Call the school and say that your child is going to be late because he has overslept and that you believe it would be a good idea if there were some definite consequences for his tardiness. When Buford arrives at school, his teacher might say, "Buford, I see you're late but you're very lucky. You're going to be able to make up that twenty minutes you missed this morning by staying in at recess and doing some work while the rest of the kids go out and play."

Granted, calling Buford's bluff and letting him sleep in and be late for school is not an easy task or prospect. It can cause you anything from embarrassment to inconvenience. For example, you may have to drive Buford to his school because the bus will not be available by the time he's ready.

(On the other hand, if the school is anywhere within walking distance, let Buford be the one who's inconvenienced—let him walk.)

Winning the "can't get 'em up in the morning" battle may be tough, but if you persevere for a few days or possibly a week or two, it will pay off. The choice is yours—you can remain a human alarm clock and take the responsibilities that really belong to your child, or you can turn those responsibilities over to him and let him be accountable for getting up in the morning.

Please note, however, that you could be one of those lucky parents who has a child who gets up at first call in the morning with no particular problems. If you are so blessed, please ignore all my advice about buying alarm clocks and continue in your bliss. Later, as the child grows older, he may want his own alarm clock, but it will be for his own convenience, not as a disciplinary measure.

Homework

Getting children to do their homework is a problem as early as third grade in many school systems across the country. Most teachers I talk to tell me that if the child is efficient at all with the use of his time, he can get most of his homework done during free time while still at school. Of course, many children prefer to play or fritter away the minutes in other ways, and they have to bring the homework home.

And there's where the battle starts. For parents who are involved in their child's homework problems, I suggest several basic steps:

1. *Remembering a basic reality discipline principle, they do not try to "make" their child do his homework.* What they should do is try to provide an environment conducive to study time.

In some homes that is all Mom and Dad really need to do. Some children are self-directed enough to want to do a good job on their homework and with a little cooperation from Mom or Dad, they finish it in good order.

If possible, provide a special study room, but if this is a luxury that isn't available, the child's bedroom is usually the place he will study. He should have a desk and some space where he can spread out his books and papers.

It is also a good idea to allot certain times for children to do their schoolwork. After dinner, from 6:30 to 8:00 P.M., Mondays through Thursdays, would be appropriate for the fourth through the eighth grade. Younger children would benefit from the same schedule but with less time, perhaps 6:30 to 7:00 or 7:15 P.M. Of course this will vary according to family circumstances.

Mom can cooperate by being mindful that while little Buford is studying, she should make a concentrated effort to be as quiet as possible. Running the vacuum cleaner, for example, isn't going to help get the homework done.

2. *Another critical point that many parents have to consider is that they should not do the child's homework for him.* Some people chuckle at the concept of a parent doing the child's homework, but I have known many parents who have done exactly that—on a regular basis. (Some of the worst offenders are parents who are also teachers. After dinner they turn the home into a pseudoschoolhouse.)

I strongly urge parents to back off and refuse to get involved in homework to any great degree. If a child asks for help with his work occasionally, that's another matter. But everyone has to understand that "occasionally" means exactly that. If you don't watch it, you will soon be sucked into a situation where you spend most of your evening hours through the week with your child's schoolwork. If that has been happening to you, something is wrong. Get together with the child's teacher or counselor and talk about it. Make a commitment to stay out of your child's schoolwork and to assist the teacher in every way you can in getting the child to do his own work.

This can sometimes be difficult for parents because they have a natural inclination to want to help the child (who may be having some genuine difficulties). And, there is always the factor of parental pride—the embarrassment of having little Buford push C's and D's when the parent knows he could help him get B's and maybe even an A.

So, my rule of thumb is: some help, yes; a lot of help, no; continual help, never! For example, if your child comes and asks you to drill him on his spelling words, go ahead and do so. That takes a relatively short amount of time and falls into the category of real help and not just doing his work for him. And, it helps show your child that you are interested in what he is doing.

3. *But suppose your child just isn't getting into his homework.* Suppose you have provided the study space and have made every effort to keep the house quiet, and your child still isn't getting the homework assignments done. Your next step would be to create some logical consequences (see chapter 7). The best way to use logical consequences is by talking with your child and letting him help set the consequences.

For example, if his homework is not done and his grades are not C or better, he will not be able to go out to play after school or after supper. He may not engage in extracurricular activities or sports such as Little League. I repeat, talk with your child about what he thinks would be fair and work out something that sounds reasonable to both of you.

Also remember that the grades your child gets are *his* and not *yours.* Be sure to talk to your child about his grades. While looking over a poor report card you might want to comment, "I'm very sorry to see that you don't enjoy learning." This would be an honest comment but would not be critical or demeaning.

If your child seems to make little improvement, be patient. Some children do not do well in school in certain grades and then improve a great deal later on. As a Christian parent you have been given authority and responsibility by God to train your child correctly. Always teach your child the following order of responsibilities and priorities:

1. God
2. Parents
3. Home and family
4. School
5. Extracurricular activities

Peer Group

As your children get older, the peer group starts to make its presence felt. I find peer-group pressure starting with children as early as first and second grade.

In order for parents to fulfill their mission, they must realize that their children want to belong. All children have two basic choices: They can identify themselves with their family or they can identify themselves with their peer group—the other kids on the block or at school. Rest assured, however, that your children will belong somewhere.

The challenge for parents is to communicate daily to their children that they belong in the family. Feelings of belonging are one of the key building blocks of self-esteem. If your child feels he is building self-esteem at home, he is much less likely to be influenced by his peer group. Here are some simple things you can do to make your child feel, "I belong. Mom and Dad really love me."

1. *Let your children have a say in planning family activities, outings, trips, and vacations.* Solicit their opinions on what they would like to do. Be willing to meet them halfway.

2. *Ask for their opinions about problems you—the parents and other members of the family—are facing.* These problems might be spiritual, financial, or emotional. When you ask for their

ideas, you are saying, "I value your opinion. You are worthwhile and important in this family."

3. *I believe we also tell children they belong when we give them work to do within the family structure.* Don't assign chores as if they are distasteful tasks everyone is stuck with. Help your children see that doing chores well is a way of taking pride in how the house looks. Granted, the appearance of the house won't be too high on their priority list until perhaps a few years later. But as they start having friends come over—particularly when they reach junior high school level and start interacting more with the opposite sex—they may make a radical improvement. Indeed, little Festus may turn into a junior-high version of Mr. Clean to make the house presentable for visits by his friends.

4. *Let your child test the system (the family's rules) and be willing to engage in give-and-take.* Eradicate from your vocabulary such phrases as, "You do it because I said so," or, "As long as you live here, you'll do it our way." Instead, be willing to reason with your child and explain *why* you believe and do *what* you believe and do. By taking time to give reasons for rules, you are saying to the child in still another way, "I value you as a person. I am paying you the compliment of treating you like someone who can think for himself."

If you want to do some further reading in the area of peer-group pressure, I suggest the following three books. Each author takes a little different slant, but all three books give key insights on the realities of what your child is facing already or will very soon be facing from his peers, and how you can make him feel more secure and accepted at home:

> *How to Really Love Your Teenager* by Ross Campbell (Chariot Victor)
>
> *Preparing for Adolescence* by James Dobson (Gospel Light)
>
> *Right from Wrong* by Josh McDowell (Word)

Potty Training

Toilet training your child is one task that probably requires more reality discipline for you than it does for your child. We all know the lady whose child was potty trained at ten months or fourteen months. In many cases, the child hasn't been potty trained—the mother has. As long as she remembers to put the child on the potty, she probably experiences few accidents. Of course, there are exceptional children who do learn to use the potty at a very young age, but there is no rule of thumb. There is no magic day when every child should take his postgraduate course in bodily elimination.

Each of our children is unique. Each has his own time to learn to be toilet trained. Most children can start somewhere between eighteen months and two years. Be sure that you as well as your child are ready for the experience.

I tell parents—especially mothers—that the key to potty training is to remain relaxed and calm. Don't get uptight and tense. Your child will sense your feelings and get uptight and tense right along with you.

My wife and I both remember the day she announced to one of our daughters, "This is the day you're going to be toilet trained." Sande had become tired of dirty diapers and had decided that the whole situation needed some "discipline." Of course, this approach to discipline met with total disaster. Our daughter sensed Sande's tension and responded appropriately. The entire operation was a total failure, despite my wife's use of a reward system which included giving our daughter some candy every time she got near or on the potty. Where did my wife learn about using candy as a reward? You guessed it. From a book written on toilet training by—you guessed it again—a psychologist!

After the first debacle everybody forgot about toilet training and relaxed for a few months. When our daughter was about two years old, my wife thought it was time to try again.

This time she followed the advice of her *favorite* psychologist (me). She bought a plastic training potty and simply left it in the bathroom. Our daughter "discovered" the potty and started using it with great enthusiasm. In three days she was totally trained. We did reinforce her learning with a reward— some frilly underwear (for my daughter, not my wife).

I always caution parents that when it comes to potty training, children can exercise a great deal of control over adults. They begin to feel a certain amount of power over the big people who up until then have controlled their lives. When you think about it, it's not too hard to understand why a child gets these ideas of power. We really do act rather silly and say some silly things after a child has gone potty. Reinforce the child, yes; but to say, "Ohhhh, would you look at that!" or "Look at the pretty present Festus gave to Mommy," is really making far too much out of a basic act.

Some parents try to train their children by using a contraption that fits on top of a full-size toilet. A far better approach is to get your child a potty chair, the kind that sits on the floor and is the child's size. He can sit on it without any fear of falling. If your first attempts fail and the child isn't interested, you may want to just put the chair away for a month and then try later.

Or you may want to take the approach that I prefer. I think the best way to toilet train a child is to buy the little potty chair, put it in the bathroom, and don't ever mention a word about it. Let the child discover the potty chair for himself. If he uses it appropriately, encourage him. Hold him, talk to him, and communicate that he is really getting big and learning to act grown-up.

Entire books have been written on how to toilet train children. If you feel the need for more ideas on how to go about it, contact your pediatrician. The major principle of reality discipline that you want to use in toilet training is to relax, be calm, and let nature take its course. There isn't a more natural act in the entire world and your child will learn when

209

he or she is ready. Whatever you do, never be intimidated or fooled by claims from other mothers who have read some book about "toilet training in less than one hour." Believe me, that is *not* reality.

Sibling Rivalry

Few families with more than one child escape problems with sibling rivalry. I believe that part of the problem arises from the tendency for parents to feel that all children have to be treated the same. At least you can be sure that's what the children try to convey. What one child gets, the other child wants.

My own children tried to work me along these lines on different occasions. Holly would say, "Daddy, how come she got that and I didn't get that? How come Krissy can do that and I can't?"

Sometimes I would tease Holly a little and "pull the rug" by saying something outlandish like, "Well, obviously it's because your mother and I love her so much more than we love you!"

If Holly continued to pester me and demand equal treatment, I would finally challenge her with something like this: "Okay, Holly, if you really want me to treat you exactly like your little sister, Krissy, your bedtime is now 8:30 instead of 9:00 P.M. and your allowance is two dollars and fifty cents instead of three dollars."

At this point Holly would decide she really didn't want to be treated the same in all circumstances. The above illustration worked quite nicely for me because in that case Holly was older than Krissy and already was receiving more privileges, such as a later bedtime and a larger allowance. We had allowed Krissy to do something that Holly thought she could do too, and that is what caused the problem. But what happens if a younger child wants the same privileges that his older brother or sister is getting? The principle of reality discipline to always invoke is that you love all your children equally but you treat them differently, according to what you believe is appropriate and fair at the time.

One of the major forces behind sibling rivalry is that our kids want the best of both worlds. They want to be sure that brother or sister doesn't get more than they do, but at the same time they want to be treated differently—as someone special. It's too easy for parents to fall into the trap of having to play judge and jury.

Much of what I mentioned under "Fighting" applies to sibling rivalry. As I said in that section, you cannot fully eliminate rivalry between siblings; you should try to find ways to minimize and control it. In fact, allowing a child to vent frustrations and feelings about a sibling is healthy and will in the long run defuse hostility, anger, and chronic rivalry.

Obviously, the trick is to keep it under control and not let it get out of hand. The basic principle of reality discipline to use with sibling rivalry is to always try to get your children to work out situations and disagreements among themselves if at all possible. For example, if two children, seven and nine years old, are having a hassle, remove them from the family room and put them in a room alone with instructions to stay in there until they can work things out.

Always remember that much of the verbal clawing that goes on among siblings is for the benefit of their parents. They want us to intervene and get involved. One child takes a cheap shot at his brother or sister and gets a derogatory response in return and before you know it, the whole family is in the middle of a war. If kids want to be miserable, if they want to yell and scream at each other, they can do it outside of the house or in some room at the other end of the house. They are not to do it at the dinner table or in the family room.

Another key reality discipline principle to remember is that children will consciously or unconsciously lay traps for their parents to attempt to get them into their arguments and disagreements and involve their parents in solving the problem. The responsible parent, however, uses reality discipline to stand back and allow the children to work out their own difficulties, if at all possible.

In traditional homes where reward and punishment are the rule, children often try to set each other up. They want the parents to intervene and pass down some kind of judgment to punish a brother or sister. This kind of "judge and jury" game usually has a 50 percent accuracy rate at best and usually creates more chaos and ill will than it solves.

In my counseling practice I've heard many youngest-child reports about how they enjoyed setting up an older sibling and pushing the right buttons to get older brother or sister to hit them. Then, with perfect timing and theatrical skills worthy of an Academy Award, this youngest child would scream, whine, or yell in such a way to make the parent believe that death was imminent. Usually, the parent's reaction was to punish the older brother or sister swiftly and aggressively. Although the younger child had to bear the pain of getting hit a few times by the older brother or sister, he always felt it was worth it. Why? Because he truly enjoyed watching the parent wale the older brother or sister.

We psychologists frequently counsel family situations where we see the oldest child going through life seemingly "looking over his shoulder" at the siblings who are closing in behind. The technical word for this is *dethronement*. The dethronement problem is always more pronounced when siblings are close in age, and it is heightened when siblings are of the same sex.

While it may not be perfect in every situation, I still believe that the best system to insure individual and fair treatment of children is to "grant the birthright" to the eldest child. This means the eldest child has more freedom and privileges, but he or she also has more responsibilities.

The TV Monster

Television is a growing problem for parents today. The channels are full of garbage that ranges from violence and immoral sex to just plain poor programming and poor taste. And it's not only what they see on TV that disturbs me, but what they don't see. Show me a program where men are depicted as anything other than bumbling buffoons, a program where Mom and Dad honor and respect each other, where kids respect the authority of anyone including their parents, or where the tragic results of casual sex are shown. Even programs that don't explicitly present bad language, sex, or violence often *do* violence to our ideas of what family life should be.

But while TV is a problem, it also presents an opportunity for using reality discipline effectively. Here are some steps that you should take.

1. *Construct guidelines for watching television in your family.* Find out what your kids want to watch and view some of these programs yourself. If some of them are not acceptable, tell your children what your feelings are and explain why you feel the way you do.

The term *acceptable* is extremely subjective. The important thing is that you come up with basic guidelines for what is acceptable TV in your home, and then stick with those guidelines.

2. *Another important factor is to limit the time your children spend watching television.* Always stress the reality discipline idea that work still comes before play and homework is done before TV is even an option.

3. *Monitor your children's program selection even if you can't always be there.* Devices are already being marketed that allow the parent to preselect television programming for as much as a week at a time. This kind of gadget is especially helpful

213

in single-parent homes where children have to be by themselves for longer periods of time.

4. *Do some homework with the* TV Guide *each week.* Identify TV programs or specials that are worthwhile for the entire family. Make it a big event. Pop a little corn and enjoy it together. May I suggest finding our TV show *realFAMILIES.* I cohost the show with Dr. Jay Passavant. It's live with an audience and lots of fun. Come find us!

5. *Acquaint yourself with other viewing options.* I've heard Christian parents complain about cable TV, but I'll take cable any day. While networks are showing insipid and suggestive shows, cable has informative programming for the whole family. Besides several cable networks that target kids specifically, many cable and satellite TV systems offer Christian programming on networks such as CBN and PAX. And take a look at the children's videos available from Christian and other wholesome sources. From *Veggie Tales* to the Disney classics, you should find tapes that teach and entertain in a positive way.

Traveling Terrors

Suppose you are planning to travel across country on your annual vacation. Regarding your children, you can: (a) leave them home; (b) send them to camp; (c) take them along; (d) send them ahead UPS. If the answer is c (take them along), you probably already know that traveling with children is difficult.

One surefire way to get there without problems is to carry them "deer style" on the front of the car. If you are old enough to remember that cars used to have fenders, perhaps you can picture little Buford and Festus strapped up there above the headlights, guaranteeing you will arrive without any fighting, bickering, or forty-seven pit stops. But since you probably don't have the fenders or the heart for such a radical solution, I suggest you keep the following basics in mind as you travel with your children:

1. *If you have young children (five years old and under), tape record all of their favorite stories.* They can spend hours listening and while you may get a little bored by endless reruns of Dr. Seuss or Baby Moses, it is infinitely better than listening to bickering and whining. Also, bring along a blank tape or two and let your kids do some recording of their own. They love to hear the sound of their own voices.

2. *Kids frequently ask for something to eat or drink.* A wise parent brings along some popcorn. It's great roughage for kids. It does make a mess, but it is easy to vacuum up later. Popcorn is much better than chocolate bars. It's healthier and won't stain (as long as you go easy on the butter).

Also take along something nutritious to drink. Kids get enough sugar poured into their bodies. Diet drinks are as bad or worse because of the chemicals. Little cans of apple or pineapple juice are perfect, as is bottled water.

3. *Many parents are aware of standard traveling games like counting telephone poles, cows, and so on.* Another old standby is finding license plates from other states. Another excellent "pass the time" gimmick is a "grab bag" or oatmeal box containing *washable, nontoxic* markers and some pads of paper. *Do not bring crayons.* They will melt in the sun and cause disaster in cars.

Another good product to bring along, especially for kids under five years old, is Colorforms—little plastic cutout figures that adhere to the car windows. They are ideal for use in cars and even on trains and planes because they are easily removed later. Kids can amuse themselves for hours with Big Bird, Yogi Bear, and dozens of other familiar cartoon characters.

4. *The "I need to go potty" cry is bound to be heard—usually every few miles.* One way to keep the potty cry down to a minimum is this: Every time you stop, for any reason, take the child to look at the rest room. Kids are fascinated by rest

rooms. They love to just look them over, whether they want to use them or not. And one out of two times they probably will want to use them. All of this helps eliminate some of the pit stops that parents find themselves making.

5. *Avoid making promises while traveling.* Don't promise your children anything. There is no reason to do so and it can get you in all kinds of difficulties. Promising them it won't rain, or that "we will be there by noon," can give you figurative and literal headaches. Kids have memories like elephants and you don't need mile after mile of, "But you promised. . . ."

6. *Don't spit on your children.* I know that sounds a little off the wall, but I am serious. Many parents find themselves in situations where they need to get the children cleaned up. Because they have nothing handy they use their own saliva, with a hankie, to clean off Buford's face. If there is any horrifying memory I have of my own childhood, it is having Mommy's saliva all over my face.

Instead of spitting on your kids, take a Tupperware or other container full of wet washcloths or buy packages of Wet Ones.

The name of all of the above games is "diversionary tactics." It is frustrating (maddening as the day wears on) to have children crawling all over themselves and you and demanding Mommy's and Daddy's attention. These ideas are designed to help children amuse themselves and give their parents a break. With a little preplanning and preparation, you can make that trip across country with the kids far more pleasant—for you and for them.

Twelve

Winning Ways

Nowadays they train some soldiers with high-tech computer games. The story is told of one recruit who was amassing huge scores in a tank-warfare simulation. His commander came by to observe the young prodigy and immediately spotted a problem.

"You're gunning down your own troops, son."

"Yeah," the soldier replied, his fingers still on the firing button, "but I'm winning this way."

Sometimes parents work so hard to "win" at parenting that they shoot down their own troops—the children. Yes, you have to stick to your guns, even when your kids think up a million reasons for you to change your mind. But ultimate victory comes not in proving yourself right but in building your children into people who can deal with the realities of life.

In the daily grind of parenting, you'll face lots of tough decisions. We've examined common behaviors of children and the family situations that often become battlegrounds. In this chapter, I focus on general parenting strategies you might use to apply reality discipline in your home (and a few strategies you should avoid).

Active Listening

Reality discipline is based on action but it is also based on listening. When a problem arises, the very first thing you want to do is listen. Suppose your nine-year-old is stomping his feet and raging about his friend down the street, his teacher, or maybe his soccer coach. What are you to say? What could really help?

When you actively listen to your child, you don't correct him, lecture him, or threaten him. You simply let him know that you can see he's got a problem. You can say something like, "Hey, you look upset. Do you want to talk about it?"

If a child stomps out of the room and slams his bedroom door, you can make a pretty good guess that he doesn't want to talk about it right now. In a while, maybe half an hour, he'll come out and be contrite and willing to take up your offer.

When a child indicates he is willing to talk, your second step is to respond to his feelings. For example, the child may say, "You never let me do anything!"

An appropriate response from you that would let a child know you are aware of his feelings would be something like, "You're angry and upset with me." A nonproductive, unhealthy way to respond to a child's comment, "You never let me do anything," would be something like, "Don't you ever talk to me like that, young man. Don't you know who I am—I'm your mother!"

What should a parent say when the child says, "I can't do it, Mommy"? The parent who has not actively listened to the child's feelings would make a discouraging response, something along the lines of, "Of course you can do it. You just did the same thing last week." But when you are actively listening to feelings, an encouraging response might be, "It really seems hard for you."

It seems natural for most parents to feel that their first duty is to correct their child or lecture in some way in order to give the right solution or point out the right answer. As you cultivate the skill of active listening, you will do less and less lecturing and giving of right answers. You will resist the temptation to try to readily solve all the problems in your child's life. And you will do more and more empathizing— letting your child know that you understand how he feels and that you care about his feelings.

Anger

A common question I am asked at my Family Living seminars throughout the country is, "Should a parent ever get angry?"

Of course parents should get angry! The question is, should we get angry at our child or at what our child does? When we begin to draw that fine line, we can see a much greater difference in the effect our anger will have.

Parents need the liberty of getting angry at what a child does. For example, suppose you have just cleaned the house and you find that your five-year-old has hauled out all his toys and left them in the living room. At a time like this it would be very appropriate for you to exercise your lungs and at the same time communicate how angry you are about the situation. The trick is in how you communicate your anger. You might use a statement like, "I feel so angry when I look at those toys scattered throughout the living room. I just spent two hours this morning cleaning up the house. I could just scream!"

Now that is an honest statement about how Mom might feel about a five-year-old's irresponsible behavior. Has Mom communicated that she doesn't love her child? No, she hasn't. She has simply sent him an "I" message that tells him she has angry feelings. She has not sent him any kind of "you" message that says, "You are a naughty child. I can't stand having you around."

Granted, it would be a good idea for Mom to sit down with her five-year-old (after he gets all of his toys picked up) and do a little more communicating. She could explain some of her feelings of anger and frustration. She could try to help him understand that she works hard to get the house straightened up and when he messes it up, it is very discouraging to her. All of this should be done with the five-year-old on Mom's lap, eyeball to eyeball, all the time holding and touching the child and reaffirming the fact that he is loved and accepted.

For more on handling anger and centering on the behavior and not the child see "Communication" on page 224.

Comforting

Parents often face a child who is distressed, unhappy, or crying over one problem or another. When does reality discipline say to go ahead and comfort and when should a different approach be used?

For example, what do you do when a child comes home crying over a bad report card? A healthy statement from Mom or Dad could be something like this: "You feel bad about your grades and you are discouraged. You're afraid that Mommy and Daddy will think less of you because you got bad grades." Obviously, an unhealthy response would be something like this: "You *ought* to be crying, with grades like that. I'd be ashamed to bring them home to my parents. In my day . . ."

As soon as you use the words *in my day* you have turned off the communication valve in your child's mind. By showing disapproval of the bad grades, you have also only reinforced his fears and reason for crying.

When problems arise that cause your child to cry, here are some basic steps to take:

1. *Listen.* Listen carefully for what the child is saying and, more importantly, what the child is *feeling.*

2. *Respond to the child's feelings.* For example, in the healthy statement mentioned above the parent said, "You feel bad about your grades and are discouraged." This kind of comment tells the child that you know how he feels. The best thing you can show to your child is not sympathy but empathy—letting your son or daughter know that you have a fairly good idea of how he feels and that maybe you've felt that way yourself sometimes.

3. *Never be afraid to touch your child.* Touching communicates that you understand and that you care. In many cases, a touch is worth many words.

Early in my career I learned that when a child feels under pressure he may cry. He often cries through previously learned behavior. He knows that when things get tough all he has to do is shed some tears and adults back off.

Several years ago, I was demonstrating some family counseling techniques to other teachers and counselors in a group situation. I had nearly one hundred people watching me work with a real family. I was working with a boy about eight years old and I could see he was about to cry. I didn't break stride in what I was saying. I simply reached over and touched his leg. The child sniffed a few times, pulled himself together, and we were able to continue the counseling demonstration.

I'm sure, however, that if I had stopped and shown concern over his teary eyes he would have started to shed real tears and the whole session would have had to come to a halt. Chances of getting the session going again would have been very slim.

By touching the child, however, I said to him, "Hey, I understand. I understand this is tough. I understand how you're feeling. You're not feeling real good right now but we're going to go on because we need to work this problem through."

Parents can often do the same thing with their children. A simple touch lets them know that you understand.

4. *Always look for alternatives.* In many cases a parent sees the child crying, hears the complaint, and is tempted to solve the problem quickly and easily from the adult point of view. Reality discipline prefers to help the child solve her own problem, if possible. Think of alternatives that you can mention and urge your child to think of alternatives as well. For example, suppose the family plans a picnic on Saturday, but everyone awakens to a torrential rainstorm. The picnic is ruined and your child starts to cry and carry on.

Hold the child close and show your own disappointment, but then ask the child if she can think of some alternatives. Perhaps you can have a picnic another day. If the child is young, waiting will not appeal too much. Perhaps you can have a picnic at home. (Be sure you have space to create a picnic setting in your family room!)

Whatever you do, do not chastise the child for her disappointment. But at the same time, do not simply give her the adult solution or reasoning such as, "Well, rainstorms happen. We'll just have to wait for another day."

5. *Give the child a choice.* After looking at all the alternatives, let the child choose—don't make the choice for him. When you make choices for your child, you are actually being disrespectful. Reality discipline always trains the child to make his own choices in a responsible way.

6. *Never accept excuses.* When you begin to accept the child's excuses, you are really tempting him to always point his finger in some other direction than at himself. You encourage him to always find the fault elsewhere and not to face his own responsibilities.

7. *See your child's mistakes as building blocks, not as defeats or frustrations.* She learns from mistakes and so can you. Reality discipline always teaches that the failures and mistakes of life are not negative but positive. They are important helps to learning how to improve and do better next time.

8. *Encourage commitment.* If you're working a problem through with your child, get a commitment from him to solve the problem through his own strength and efforts.

9. *Be ready to reevaluate the problem after the child tries to pick out a solution.* You may want to do this at several intermediate steps. Don't let the child flounder in failure. Always show your willingness to stand by her and give appropriate help when needed. The first rule, however, is to let the child try to work it out herself.

I recall one occasion when Sande and I took our three oldest children to the public library. Holly was in the fourth grade and needed, some help with finding reference works, such as an encyclopedia. She started asking us to help her, but we gently suggested that she talk to the librarian and have the librarian show her how to find various reference works. Krissy and Kevin went their way to find the books they liked, while Sande and I browsed to find books that we were interested in.

Meanwhile, Holly did talk to the librarian and got the help she needed, and everything went beautifully. I believe, however, that if we had tried to help Holly find what she was looking for, it would have ended in some kind of hassle. Furthermore, she would not have learned how to use a library and how to get the librarian's help.

Communication

Without good communication, the action-oriented techniques of reality discipline will have limited results. The following are eight principles or rules for good communication with your children.

1. *Think before you speak.* Strive to accept your child as unconditionally as possible. Meet your child where he lives. Jesus always met people on their ground and dealt with them according to their needs. Always look for ways you can develop door openers with your children. Some of the simplest and best ones are, "Do you know, honey, I could be wrong, but . . ." Or, "I could be way out in left field on this, but . . ." These few words do much to put your children in a receptive mood. They are much more likely to listen to what you have to say because you are not coming on strong or in a threatening way.

2. *Stress the positive.* Make encouraging statements and compliments "second nature" in your conversation. Always look for encouraging ways to interact with your children. Stressing the positive is just as easy as stressing the negative. Emphasizing the positive side takes no longer than the negative and the results are so much better. For example, your daughter is in a gymnastics meet and she scores very well in five events and poorly in one. You could say, "In those five events where you scored so well, you looked like you were having a great time and really enjoying yourself. You really did a good job. Congratulations." There is no need to even mention the event in which she did poorly. If she brings it up, you can say, "Yes, that one was tougher for you, but practice hard and you'll do better next time. I really like what you did in those other five events. I thought you were especially good on the balance beam."

3. *When you have to deal with the negative, do it in a positive, matter-of-fact way.* For one idea on how to handle this, see point 2

above and the suggested concern over doing poorly in one of the gymnastics events. Another example can be your four-year-old coming home with something that doesn't belong to him. It's obvious that he picked it up in your neighbor's yard. Do not berate him, lecture him, or carry on as if he were Public Enemy Number One. Simply say in a matter-of-fact way, "That doesn't belong to you, Buford. Let's take it back to the owner."

Then take Buford by the hand, walk him over to your neighbor's house, and have him return the item. Suggest to him that he say he is sorry he took it and that he won't do it again. On the way back home, say something like, "I'll bet you feel good about taking that back. Why don't we go play on the swings for a while?"

4. *Take time with your child.* Taking time with your child *communicates* that you really care. And I'm talking about special time—one on one—with each child each week. That's a tall order for most of us—but oh, so worthwhile. Mom and Dad should talk together about how they can help each other get away for one-on-one sessions with each of the children. Yes, it will be a lot of trouble, but I repeat, it will make a tremendous difference.

5. *Always be aware that you don't have to like what your child does but you should always communicate that you love him and care about him.* Some simple things you can say include: "I want you to know that I'm very unhappy when you talk to me that way. I love you and care about you so much that I feel terrible when you speak like that. I know you are upset, but I don't think we should ever talk that way to each other—even when we're angry. What do you think?"

"Do you know why I yelled so loud for you to stop when you were running into the street? If a car hit you and killed you, I would be very, very sad. I love you too much to have anything like that happen."

When children misbehave, anger is a natural feeling. You do not have to be afraid to express your anger. But you must remember that your anger needs to be focused on the act or the behavior and not on the child.

6. *When you "blow it" with your children, ask their forgiveness.* This will accomplish two things. First, you will achieve much better communication with your children. Second, you will model how to ask forgiveness and help your children learn this difficult art.

When admitting your mistakes, start your statements with phrases such as, "I was wrong . . ." "I owe you an apology . . ." "I used poor judgment . . ." "I wasn't using my head . . ." All of these phrases show the child your transparency and willingness to admit your imperfections. Do not worry that your child will lose respect for you under these circumstances. On the contrary, precisely the opposite will happen.

7. *Keep in mind that results aren't always evident over the short term.* Parenthood is for the long haul. It is a long-range investment. If your child doesn't always respond to the techniques of reality discipline, don't give up. You are going to discipline your child in one way or another, regardless of the results, and you might as well be using a system that is based on Scripture (Eph. 6:4), which will pay off in the long run.

8. *Ask for God's guidance daily, in your own life as well as in the lives of your children.* Let your prayer be that God's goodness will shine through your life in such a way that children will see the reality of your personal relationship with the Almighty God.

Cooperation

Mothers in particular constantly ask me how they can get their children to cooperate more with doing chores, being on time, and so on. I believe reality discipline is the perfect tool for getting the child's attention and pointing out the need for cooperation in the home in a swift and direct manner. One basic approach is to teach the child that if he doesn't cooperate with you, you may not necessarily cooperate with him. This is the reality that he will always face in life, whether it be at school or later when he is grown up and has his own job and family.

I recall working with a mother whose little four-year-old would use whining, crying, and fussing as a way of keeping himself in control of situations at home. One afternoon, the mother asked her little boy to pick up his toys. It was a reasonable request. There weren't that many lying around and he knew exactly where they should go. But little Jimmy responded with, "They're too heavy."

At the time, Mom was fighting a deadline—she had a dentist appointment. She left the toys on the floor untouched and took the child with her to the dentist.

On the way home from the dentist, Jimmy began working on Mom for an ice-cream treat. But as they drove by the ice-cream stand, Mom turned to Jimmy and said quietly, "Honey, you can't have a treat today. You still have responsibilities left to do at home. I'm talking about your toys."

When they arrived home, there were the toys, lying where they had been left. Jimmy got the message. He picked up his toys and put them away.

In this simple incident we see reality discipline being demonstrated in several basic ways:

1. The mother loved the child so much that she wouldn't succumb to his every whim.
2. She would not be used or manipulated by the child. She was in authority over the child and no vice versa.
3. She did not "snowplow" the roads of life for her child by doing his work for him. If the mother had picked up the toys herself (which she could easily have done much faster), she would have been training him to be irresponsible.

4. The incident taught her son a basic lesson in cooperation—don't cooperate with Mom and Mom can't
cooperate with you. The key point here, however, is
not the "eye for an eye" concept as much as it is teaching the child that when you don't meet your responsibilities you can't have things your way.

Suppose the four-year-old had arrived home but still
didn't want to pick up his toys. The mother could have
invoked reality discipline in further ways by not allowing
him to do anything until his chore was satisfactorily completed. There would have been no playing, no television, no
snacks or treats. Reality discipline stresses order, that A (the
responsibility) comes before B (the reward or the treat).

Another important point is that the mother was quiet but
firm. She did not shout at the child or verbally abuse him.
You can try to shout or even beat your children into cooperating with you and at times you may think you are suc-
ceeding. But obtaining obedience through intimidation,
nagging, and fear is not the way to cooperation. It is the way
to teach your child to intimidate others as he gets older.
With reality discipline, you are always seeking to respect
your child as well as yourself. You are always trying to show
your child that cooperation is a two-way street, not a one-
way thoroughfare on which he does all the joyriding.

Encouragement

As I deal with parents, I see many of them who find it difficult to grasp the difference between giving their child
encouragement and giving praise. After all, many books tell
parents to compliment and praise their children often.
Indeed, one of the problems in too many homes is that too
many children never get any compliments or praise to speak

of; they are usually criticized or told what they didn't do rather than what they did well.

I understand the motivation behind admonishing parents to praise their children, but I prefer to stress the need for encouragement rather than praise. It is difficult to understand but praise can be very discouraging. In the ultimate sense, only God is worthy of praise. People need encouragement, not praise.

Encouragement centers on a person's efforts, improvement, sense of responsibility, tenacity, and appreciation for progress. Examples of encouraging words to your children are these:

"I'm sure you can handle it."

"I'm glad to see you enjoy learning."

"How thoughtful of you—the kitchen looks great!"

"Now you're getting it!"

"You looked as if you were having a great time in the game today."

"It looks as if that extra practice really paid off for you—congratulations!"

"How do you feel? You've come a long way."

By contrast, statements of praise sound like this:

"My, you're a good boy."

"Mommy is so proud of you, dear. You did so well in the recital tonight."

"You ate all your dinner. What a good girl! Now you can have dessert."

"Three A's and a B! That makes me so happy. Now next time, let's get that B up to an A!"

"Your behavior was great at the scout meeting tonight. Here's five dollars to show you how much it meant to me."

As I mentioned earlier, in *Parenthood without Hassles— Well, Almost,* I included what I called "A Child's Ten Commandments to Parents." All of these "commandments" are written in the words of a young child to his parents. One of them says: "I need your encouragement, but not your praise, to grow. Please go easy on the criticism; remember, you can criticize *the things I do* without criticizing *me.*"

I encourage all parents to be aware of what they are saying to their children. Are your remarks more in the form of praise or are you learning how to encourage instead? The difference is subtle but vitally important. Praise can actually defeat and deflate a person's sense of self-worth, particularly a child's. Praise suggests *qualified* love. It triggers in a child's mind the questions, *Am I loved and praised because I got good grades or cleaned the kitchen? What would happen if I didn't do those things?*

Love

This suggestion almost seems unnecessary, yet I deal with parents all the time who find it difficult to tell their children, "I love you." Perhaps these parents were brought up in homes where they weren't told they were loved and it is difficult for them to share their intimate thoughts and feelings with their children. But if reality discipline is to work for you the way it can, you must be able to communicate your feelings of love.

We have five children, and I can't remember a day in any of their lives, when I was in contact with them at all, when I didn't tell them, "I love you." And not only do I tell them, I show them. I can think of three ways to communicate love to a child:

1. Discipline the child. I'm not talking about punishment—I'm talking about giving the child the loving correction he or she needs at the time it is needed.
2. Touch your children. Hug them, pat them. The power of touch is incredible!

3. Show interest in what your child is interested in. So many children live their own lives while Mom and Dad, it seems, live theirs.

I've already mentioned the survey made by family counselor Craig Massey, who found that 79 percent of the twenty-two hundred children from Christian homes that he surveyed felt unloved. One survey doesn't necessarily make a total case, but nonetheless to find 79 percent of *any* group feeling unloved is mind-boggling, and when the survey is done among Christian homes, it is even more mind-boggling. How can this be? Why is it that in homes where the parents supposedly have a relationship to God in Christ, and know something of God's love, children feel unloved? I think one of the basic answers has to be that parents simply do not know how to communicate their love. They find it hard to let their children grow up and learn to make their own decisions. It may seem paradoxical, but one way to communicate your love to your child is to give your child the freedom to make decisions. And to give your child the freedom to fail. When the failures come, that's the time to really say, "I love you," and to show it with hugs and pats and smiles.

Mistakes

I'm not talking about mistakes by your kids. I mean the ones *you* make. Now what does a parent do when he makes a mistake? I know it sounds easy to lay out step-by-step ways to solve problems with your children, but I also know the feelings of frustration and failure when things don't work out perfectly. I know what it's like to have my plans and convictions and motivations go astray. Life is not perfect, and neither are we.

231

I think of the time my daughter Krissy was six years old and just learning to ride a two-wheeler bike. She got to the point where I felt she really had the ability to ride by herself without any support or extra help. She would take a couple of steps, jump on her bike, pedal a couple of times, and then jump off. It seemed that all she needed was the confidence to stay on and keep going.

So, one Saturday morning *Dad* decided that today Krissy would learn to "really ride a bike."

My arbitrary decision that this was Krissy's day to learn what I wanted her to learn was my first mistake. I got her out in the street in the residential area where we live. I walked her along with both hands on the bike. Then she pedaled a little bit and we went up a hill and began to come down the other side. Now she was pedaling gently along and I was trotting along next to her, still balancing the bike. I had already let go for a few seconds to make sure she could balance properly and she was doing nicely. We went a few more feet and I made the decision (without checking with Krissy) to let her go the rest of the way down the hill all by herself. As I let go of her, her speed accelerated, she lost control, and veered off the street straight into a cactus bush. If you haven't noted before, we live in Tucson, Arizona, which grows some of the meanest cactus bushes in the west. Poor little Krissy went tumbling off straight into the bush and we spent quite a while picking stickers out of her little six-year-old body.

Of course, I hurt more than she did, but that didn't make Krissy feel any better. And it was a long time before Krissy got back on that bike—at least a good year.

Of course, she learned a couple of things from her experience with letting Dad teach her to ride a bike:

1. Stay away from two-wheeler bikes—they're dangerous.
2. Stay away from Dad—he's even more dangerous!

I did learn quite a bit that day, however. I learned that I had interrupted Krissy, who was learning to ride a bike in her own way and at her own speed. With all my motivation to be a good guy and a helpful daddy, I had moved in and tried to force her to go too far too fast. I tried to make her learn at my speed and it had ended in disaster.

I tell you that illustration to help you understand two things:

1. *Never force your child to do more than he or she is able to do.* When using reality discipline, it is possible to go over the line. In trying to make a child accountable and responsible, we can push the child beyond his capabilities at the time.

2. *Hold your child accountable, but don't apply unnecessary pressure.* How do you know when you are applying unnecessary pressure? There is no absolute and guaranteed way to know—you will just have to tune in to your child and communicate (see "Communication").

3. *Using reality discipline cuts both ways.* You always want the child to understand what reality is, but you also need to understand reality—especially the reality of your child's abilities, fears, and weaknesses. In short, reality discipline is always ministered with a good dose of love.

Nagging

Parents are often caught in a bind. They find themselves having to remind their children to do or not do certain things. The parent does the reminding while all the child hears is "nagging."

Reality discipline has an answer for the problem. Simply stop doing all that reminding.

Parents look at me as if I've lost my mind when I make that suggestion. They ask a very logical question: "What's wrong with reminding a child? Doesn't everyone need a reminder once in a while?"

Yes, I'm sure most human beings need to be reminded of things now and then, but the problem with parents is that they have let it get out of hand. The pattern, in many homes, is that Mom and Dad constantly remind or coax the children to do things they are expected to do on a regular and routine basis. I tell parents to stop this pattern of reminding and coaxing. When you continue to remind and coax your child to do things that he knows he is supposed to do, you are teaching him to be irresponsible.

For example, when you constantly have to coax or remind a child to come to dinner, you are simply teaching him that the first call doesn't matter. He can continue watching TV, playing, or building his model airplane and Mom will continue to call three or four more times. When the decibel level gets up to a certain intensity, then he knows he'd better come.

All of this is very hard on everyone. The choice is clear: You can train your children up to respond the first time they are asked to do things, or you can train them to not listen to the first request or warning and simply go on their merry way until they cause a problem.

So, how do you apply reality discipline to the reminding and nagging problem? Let your children know that you are going to tell them things only once. You are not going to be disrespectful to them by communicating that you think they are so stupid they cannot understand what you say the first time you say it. Tell them you are not going to repeat things over and over again. If they do not come or do not heed the first time, you will move in with actions and not words. Let them know what the consequences will be if they do not come the first time (for example, if called to dinner and they don't come, they don't get dinner). And then back up what you say.

I repeat, the choice is yours. You can deal with your children in a mentally healthy way or in an unhealthy way. To continually remind, nag, and coax is unhealthy for everyone concerned.

Time Out

By "time out" I am talking about stopping what the child is doing and making him sit down for a while—on a chair or in his room—to do some thinking.

Parents often ask me if time out is a good thing. Is it a good way to administer discipline? I always tell them that indeed it is. There are many moments through the day when Mom or Dad needs to call time out. For the benefit of the social order in the home, little Festus or Felicia needs to sit down on a chair, or go sit in his or her room and do some thinking and quieting down.

When you call time out on one of your children, you are simply telling him or her, "Your behavior is so obnoxious that you have earned the right to stay away from the rest of the family for a period of time."

When I talk about time out, I always add a word of caution. Whenever you isolate a child, don't overdo it. (Four months *is* too long, although I realize there are times when it is tempting.) Five to ten minutes is usually plenty of time for children six years old and above. Around two minutes is sufficient for preschoolers.

Keep in mind that time out is not a punishment but simply a method of helping your child understand he is responsible for his actions. When his actions become unacceptable, he has to stop and realize what he has been doing. If the child's behavior improves after time out, fine. But if he goes right back to doing the same thing that caused the original disruption or problem, you may have to call time out again.

Each time you find time out necessary, it's important to have a brief bit of communication with the child. Ask little Felicia, "How do you feel now? Are you ready to come back and play by the rules? We really want you back with the rest of the family—if you're ready."

While doing this communicating, always be sure that you touch your child. Give hugs and love as you explain why the child was isolated and why that behavior is not acceptable.

A Final Word

Children are like wet cement. There's precious little time when you can mold them into responsible, loving people. What you do in that time shapes them for the rest of their lives.

I don't say that to scare you, just to challenge you. You have an incredibly important job as a parent. I don't want to sound like a broken record, but my message is pretty simple: You *do* make a difference.

Recently I was reminded of the difference I make in the life of one of my daughters, Hannah, now 13. Her class had a writing assignment, to make analogies about their fathers, comparing their dads to some object. A number of the other kids, Hannah said, wrote things like, "My father is a rock," and went on to describe their rock-like qualities. But Hannah wrote:

> My Dad is like ice cream,
> Smooth and easy, solid and sweet,
> Full of flavor, exciting, colorful and sweet,
> Refreshing like a cool summer breeze
> Melts easy, right down to the heart
> Never boring
> Always comes in different toppings,

Makes me happy with his different toppings
Comes in a container; and he expects me to contain
   myself
There's always a little bit more

I was very touched by Hannah's analogy. It told me I'm doing something right. (Not everything, to be sure. In another page or two, I'll share one of my more glaring failures.) But we have a loving relationship that sets a context for the reality discipline I've described in this book. I've known a lot of fathers who wouldn't want to be "ice cream." They spend a lot of effort trying to be the "rock" of their home. They don't want to "melt easy, right down to the heart." I guess I'm just asking parents—both fathers and mothers—to melt a little, to be real, to show love and respect to your kids, to let your family life be "full of flavor."

In the foregoing pages I sought to give you the foundational principles of reality discipline, along with as many practical suggestions as possible for use in situations you face daily in your own family. I realize I have not covered everything. The problems in parenting are virtually limitless. What I have tried to do, however, is to touch on those major areas where parents frequently ask me for help.

I have tried to give you a basic strategy for parenting that you can modify and adapt to fit your own personality. You may not use exactly the same actions that I have suggested in every case. What is important, however, is that you do *act*—quickly and decisively—to teach your child the reality of being accountable for what he or she does.

One of the most tragic news stories I ever read was headlined, "Injured Boy Wins $810,000 Suit." The item told of how a twelve-year-old had lost part of his left foot while trying to hitch a ride on a slow-moving freight train. In handing down the $810,000 settlement the judge ruled that the boy was to start receiving monthly payments at the age of eighteen, which would continue for life. The attorney representing the lad based his argument on the charge of negligence against the city because officials knew there was a hole in the fence along the railroad tracks and *they should have known children would be tempted to go through it.*

This story is tragic for two reasons: First, a young boy was crippled for life, but even more tragic is the fact that the courts ruled in favor of irresponsibility. At age twelve a child should be able to make a much wiser decision than to climb through a fence and try to hop a freight train. The same irony is seen in an advertisement I saw years ago. The ad stated, "Don't make a kid go wrong!" The message admonishes motorists to not leave their keys in their cars because this will tempt youngsters to steal them! Is there any doubt that the time has come for reality discipline?

I'm not saying that using reality discipline gives you an ironclad guarantee that you will never have problems or that your children will never misbehave in a serious way. Reality discipline does not even guarantee that your children will become believers. But as you use the game plan and strategies that are basic to reality discipline, you will be training your children by relying on actions, not words, to help them learn to be accountable and responsible for their decisions.

Decision making—particularly the important decisions—is much harder for the child who has been allowed to run free and "do his own thing." It is equally hard for the child who has been under an authoritarian yoke where all of his decisions were made for him. But the child reared through reality discipline has had the opportunity to see what *loving authority* is all about.

I know what you may be thinking: *That sounds like a nice theory, Dr. Leman. If I had a degree in psychology I might be able to pull it off.*

Believe me, I—the so-called expert—know how difficult it can be. Kids test us constantly and we don't always pass with flying colors. I still remember an incident when Holly was well into her "terrible twos." She got into a particularly bad mood and totally defied me. Finally, I had to pick her up, put her in her room, and say, "Holly, you have to stay in here until you settle down and can behave yourself."

According to my advice to other parents (see "Time Out" in previous chapter), Holly was supposed to sit quietly for a few minutes, realize she had to be responsible for her actions, and then rejoin the family group in a much better mood. It didn't happen quite that way. In thirty seconds my tiny daughter was out of her room and right back at me, doing her best to make life less than serene. I redeposited her in her room with the same admonition: "Holly, I wish you could come back and be with Mommy and me, but you are just not ready."

I went out and closed the door, quite sure that this time Holly would get the message. But Holly was not in a message-receiving mood. This time it took *less* than thirty seconds for her to come through the door and start biting my ankles again.

The situation was becoming a bit desperate. I had already tried a swat in the proper area, but Holly's rage only increased. I decided to resort to my ultimate weapon: the Kevin Leman Memorial Doorknob. This is an ingenious invention of my own making that is simply an ordinary doorknob that has been reversed to lock on the outside. I should have used it the first time I put Holly in her room, but I had wrongly assumed that I could talk her into cooperating. With a quick flip of the lock button Holly was secure, or so I thought.

Predictably, Holly pleaded, wailed, screamed, and gave the general impression she was on a medieval torture rack. It only lasted a minute or so and then she was quiet. As I was congratulating myself for being courageous enough to use "loving authority," the doorbell rang. As fate would have it, my mother had dropped by for an unexpected visit, and she especially wanted to see Holly!

Grandma greeted me and immediately asked where her "little princess" was. I furtively glanced toward Holly's bedroom door and then almost gasped with dismay. From under the door crept tiny white fingers that mutely semaphored a plea for rescue. Grandma's keen eye instantly spotted Holly's hand, outlined on the bright-blue rug. She fixed me with a withering gaze and demanded: "You didn't lock my granddaughter in her room, did you?"

"I sure did, Mom."

Grandma gave a disgusted snort. "You, you *psychologist*, you!" was all she could manage, and she stalked away.

I stood there, staring at Holly's little fingers as they continued to send the "Mayday" message to all the world. I couldn't see her face, but I pictured her lying on her stomach, her "blankie" tucked under her arm and a smug little smile on her cherub face. I had won the battle, but I wasn't sure about the war. I waited a few more minutes and then opened the door.

"Are you ready to come out now and be part of the family?" I asked.

My two-and-a-half-year-old gave a brief nod and almost strutted past me to go find her grandma, who was sitting in the living room muttering about psychologists and what she had done to deserve a son who had become one.

When I happened to walk by a few minutes later, there was Holly, snuggled on Grandma's lap. I tried to greet them amiably, but they both gave me looks of cool disdain. I spent the rest of the day not feeling all that loving, or as if I had much authority!

I tell you that story to underscore one important point: When rearing children you will know many moments of reality when things don't go exactly by the book, whether it be this book or one written by some other child-rearing expert. My encounter with Holly and Grandma left me feeling like anything but the capable professional who handles every family crisis with fluid precision. It would be several more years before Holly would write me that precious note that I shared with you earlier. Then she would say:

My father is the gratist, for your the best, caring, Loveing, THE BEST!!!!!!

And why would she say I was the best? The last line of her note contains the secret:

even when you disaplin me, I Love you the same.

Holly didn't understand parental strategy and theories, but she could understand being disciplined with love. I have written this book to help you discipline with love as effectively as you can. You don't have to be perfect. There will be many times when you will feel frustrated and baffled. There will be times when your children or your spouse (or maybe Grandma) will send you on a guilt trip or running for cover to hide your embarrassment.

Those are the moments when you need *the courage to be imperfect,* just as I did when those tiny fingers crept out from under the door. In those moments you never give up. You stick to your game plan, always remembering that parenting is a *very* long game and one strikeout or fumble does not decide the outcome. What will decide the outcome is your commitment to train your children to be responsible and accountable for their decisions: "the loving discipline the Lord himself approves."

One More Thing

If you have a problem in your relationship with your son or daughter, here's a little suggestion that can turn a relationship around. You'll never see this suggestion anywhere else. It's an original thought based on over thirty years of working with parents and their children.

I was speaking to a group of executives in Los Angeles when a nattily dressed businessman came up to me. "Dr. Leman," he said, "I owe you an apology."

"An apology? For what?"

"Well, you spoke to our Gotham chapter [the New York chapter of the Young President's Organization], and at that time we were having all kinds of problems with our sixteen-year-old son. I asked you what we could do, and you gave us an answer, but you gave it so tersely I thought you were blowing us off."

I immediately shot back, "Oh, I know what I told you to do. I told you to stop asking questions, didn't I?"

"We finally got so desperate we tried your suggestion, and within two weeks we had a new kid on our hands."

You know, parents set the paradigm early on when they incessantly ask their children questions like:

"How was your day, honey?"

"Okay."

"What did you do in school today?"

"Nothing."

And later on, parents demand of their teenagers:

"Where have you been?"

"Out."

"What did you do?"

"Nothing."

When you back off and not become the typical hover mother or hover dad, you allow your son or daughter to begin to tell you what's going on in their lives. Parents, what you need to know is this: Kids not only *want* to belong to your family—they *need* to belong to your family. Believe it or not, they want you to approve of them, affirm them, and, of course, love them. Oh yes, and don't forget—discipline them. But remember, discipline is not something you pass down to your children. Discipline is how you live your life.

Discussion Guide

You can enhance your growth in parenting skills by conversing with other parents. Folks just like you have encountered similar challenges and struggled with the same kinds of problems with their kids. It's time to talk it over!

The following pages offer you a chance to compare notes. These pages should also help you encourage and support one another in the difficult, though highly rewarding task of raising children into happy, healthy adults. This guide will take you through three steps for reviewing and discussing each chapter of *Making Children Mind without Losing Yours.*

First, recall the chapter. This is your opportunity to think back through the chapter themes and talk about how those themes made practical impact. Give everyone a chance to explain what things "rang a bell."

Second, respond to the text. Looking at two or three quotes from the text should spark deeper discussion—or even a bit of controversy.

Third, reflect together. Here you'll find specific questions related to points made in the chapter. Choose any or all, depending on the amount of time you have for your study.

Keep in mind that your discussion will flow better if you make it a goal to stay as open-ended as possible. In other words, sometimes you'll just ask for what "rang a bell" and let the time be taken up with the responses. At other times you'll want to move through the specific questions. Be sure to start and end your time in prayer and always be willing to share the leadership. (Rotating the leadership week to week is a great option.)

Why not provide a little snack too? But however you choose to use this guide, I offer my best wishes for your enjoyment and success in exploring the blessed thrills and spills of parenthood.

Remember, the goal is to be a good parent—not necessarily a great one. And here's the Midas Muffler guarantee of parenthood: If you're a good parent, you'll end up with a great kid!

—Dr. Kevin Leman

Chapter One

It's a Jungle Out There!
Grab a Vine

✔ Recall the chapter

- Choose a portion of this chapter that had particular impact on you. Tell other group members how this idea or issue "rang a bell" with you.
- What personal story or experience comes to mind in relation to these chapter themes: (1) *using principles of reality discipline with children,* or (2) *giving and receiving unconditional love?* Talk about it!

✔ Respond to the text

How do you react to the text quotations below? For each, tell *how it applies*—or could apply—to your own family situation. If possible, offer a *personal example* from your experience with the issue.

> From page 20: Don't be afraid to let your kids fail. Too many parents worry that failure will scar their children's self-esteem. As a result the parents cheat, change the rules, pretend the child didn't fail, or keep the child from trying anything new. They feel guilty for not protecting their youngsters from such failure, and that guilt propels all sorts of bad decisions.

> From page 27: God's love for us is *unconditional.* He loves us just because we are who we are, imperfect and prone to make mistakes. And he wants us to love our children in the same unconditional way. The desire to love as uncondi-

tionally as possible is prerequisite #1 for a parent who wants to practice reality discipline.

✔ Reflect together

Discuss one or more of the following, as time permits:

1. Dr. Leman begins by talking about our parenting fears. When have you most powerfully felt the fear of making a mistake with your child?
2. How can we parents *learn* from our mistakes?
3. In your opinion, to what extent does it "take a village" to raise a child? Do you agree with Dr. Leman's position on this? Explain.
4. What would you say are some of the differences between a perfect parent and a good parent?
5. How would you describe the difference between discipline and punishment? between permissiveness and loving nurture?
6. Offer a definition of reality discipline in one concise sentence. What things about this approach to child rearing make sense to you? What concerns does this approach raise?
7. As a group, see if you can name all seven principles of reality discipline (without looking back at the text). Tell which principle seems most relevant to a parenting situation you're facing at the moment.
8. Dr. Leman says: "Kids are overexposed to activities these days." Have you seen this problem in your family? How can parents deal with this?
9. How does permissiveness "create a monster"? In your own words, summarize the alternative suggested in this chapter.
10. What other *insights* came to mind from this chapter? What new *questions* surfaced for you? Do you have any *personal applications* to consider? Explain.

Chapter Two

Inconsistency—
or How to Raise a Yo-Yo

✔ Recall the chapter

- Choose a portion of this chapter that had particular impact on you. Tell other group members how this idea or issue "rang a bell" with you.
- What personal story or experience comes to mind in relation to these chapter themes: (1) *being too authoritarian or too permissive,* or (2) *finding a middle ground between the two extremes?* Talk about it!

✔ Respond to the text

How do you react to the text quotations below? For each, tell *how it applies*—or could apply—to your own family situation. If possible, offer a *personal example* from your experience with the issue.

From page 34: If you want disaster and chaos in your life, do *everything* for your children.

From page 39: My years of counseling parents and children have shown me that in a permissive environment the kids rebel. They rebel because they feel anger and hatred toward their parents for a lack of guidelines and limit setting. . . . Children want order in their lives.

From page 44: I've never heard one of my young clients (the children) mention "quality time." All a child knows is that he wants your time and your attention, whether it's to watch him do somersaults and cartwheels or to take him for a Big Mac. In trying to find time for your children, don't worry too much about how much "quality" is in it.

✔ Reflect together

Discuss one or more of the following, as time permits:

1. What is the "one, essential ingredient" for effective discipline in the home? What evidence do you see of this in your own home these days? in the home where you grew up?
2. What does "love without discipline" look like? Can you give some real-life examples?
3. When do we begin building discipline into our child's life? Why? How?
4. Why is it important for children to know that they have the right to fail? To what extent did you have this right as a child?
5. How do children learn to make decisions? learn to be responsible and accountable? How well are your own kids doing in these areas?
6. Describe some of the differences between an *authoritative* parent and an *authoritarian* one.
7. When was the last time you held your child accountable for reality, with real-life consequences, as Dr. Leman describes? Tell what happened.
8. What's the difference between *hearing* your children and *listening* to them?
9. What would it mean for you, in practical terms, to do a better job of giving yourself to your child, as Dr. Leman suggests?
10. What other *insights* came to mind from this chapter? What new *questions* surfaced for you? Do you have any *personal applications* to consider? Explain.

Chapter Three

It's All in the Eye of the Beholder

✔ Recall the chapter

- Choose a portion of this chapter that had particular impact on you. Tell other group members how this idea or issue "rang a bell" with you.
- What personal story or experience comes to mind in relation to these chapter themes: (1) *responding to your child's perceptions,* or (2) *recognizing how children learn?* Talk about it!

✔ Respond to the text

How do you react to the text quotations below? For each, tell *how it applies*—or could apply—to your own family situation. If possible, offer a *personal example* from your experience with the issue.

From page 58: However you deal with powerful and purposive behavior, always keep in mind that every time your child takes a power trip, he or she is on another expedition of learning. He is learning about reality. If he gets away with his power plays, he learns that reality is manipulating and controlling Mom and Dad as much as possible. But if his power plays bear no fruit, he learns a different kind of reality. He learns that reality is being accountable for his actions and that unacceptable behavior has no payoff.

From page 60: For some reason, we don't think children can handle the truth. We tend to "cover" when we talk with them. We don't tell them everything that goes on because we feel they are "too young to understand." Although restraint is needed in some situations, I usually encourage parents to share their real feelings, problems, and concerns.

✔ Reflect together

Discuss one or more of the following, as time permits:

1. Where are you in your family-of-origin birth order? Do you find Dr. Leman's descriptions accurate in your case? Explain.
2. How are your own children acting out the characteristics of their birth orders? How, specifically, can your insights about birth order help you be a better parent?
3. Give an example of a child learning the wrong thing through taking a "power trip." Then give an example of good learning through power trips.
4. According to Dr. Leman, what is the most important quality for a parental role model to posses? Why is this?
5. How open are you to honestly sharing your fears and anxieties with your children as they grow older? What might hold you back?
6. Look again at the three reasons it's "worth it" to risk being honest with our children. Which of these benefits do you value the most? Why?
7. Do you agree that "you can't fool a child"? What is your experience with this?
8. Dr. Leman affectionately calls children "the enemy." What does he mean? What is the most subversive thing kids try to do to parents? What are some solutions?
9. What other *insights* came to mind from this chapter? What new *questions* surfaced for you? Do you have any *personal applications* to consider? Explain.

Chapter Four

Why Reward and Punishment Don't Work

✔ Recall the chapter

- Choose a portion of this chapter that had particular impact on you. Tell other group members how this idea or issue "rang a bell" with you.
- What personal story or experience comes to mind in relation to these chapter themes: (1) *using reward and punishment,* or (2) *promoting accountability through allowances and chores?* Talk about it!

✔ Respond to the text

How do you react to the text quotations below? For each, tell *how it applies*—or could apply—to your own family situation. If possible, offer a *personal example* from your experience with the issue.

From page 69: The emphasis is on the act and not on Justin. Mom does not say, "My, you're a good boy because you cleaned up the backyard so nicely." It's always a good idea to avoid associating a child's "goodness" with how well he does a certain task.

From page 73: Punishment teaches children that because we—their parents—are bigger and stronger, we can push them around. We can force our will upon them. And because we—the parents—can get away with this, it reinforces the idea in our own minds that it's perfectly all right to force our will upon our children.

From page 81: Through their constant nagging, coaxing, and bribing, parents are teaching their children that when they grow up and get out into life there will always be somebody there to push, motivate, and reward them for their behavior. But of course, life isn't like that.

✔ Reflect together

Discuss one or more of the following, as time permits:

1. How would you describe the difference between reward and encouragement?
2. How do you create a "carrot seeker"? Do you have one in your home?
3. Spend some time creating two or three true-to-life stories that would clearly demonstrate the difference between *punishing* a child and *disciplining* a child.
4. Have someone read aloud Hebrews 12:5–11. How does God treat his children as they grow up? What principles here are transferable to your own parenting task?
5. What are the best ways to develop a sound conscience in a child?
6. Do you give your children an allowance? Why or why not? What is your reaction to Dr. Leman's guidelines for using allowances?
7. When was the last time you "nagged" your child about doing a household chore? How do you think Dr. Leman would advise you in this case?
8. What other *insights* came to mind from this chapter? What new *questions* surfaced for you? Do you have any *personal applications* to consider? Explain.

Chapter Five

"Pull the Rug Out and Let the Little Buzzards Tumble"

✔ Recall the chapter

- Choose a portion of this chapter that had particular impact on you. Tell other group members how this idea or issue "rang a bell" with you.
- What personal story or experience comes to mind in relation to these chapter themes: (1) *pulling out the rug*, or (2) *giving children choices*, or (3) *earning a child's respect*? Talk about it!

✔ Respond to the text

How do you react to the text quotations below? For each, tell *how it applies*—or could apply—to your own family situation. If possible, offer a *personal example* from your experience with the issue.

> From page 88: Parents have been sold a bill of goods. They have heard that psychologists believe a child's psyche is so fragile that we shouldn't hurt or upset the child in any way. . . . To say they are too delicate to learn from discipline based on love and reality is foolish.

> From page 102: I believe home should be the place to make good or poor choices. The last place home should be is a place where you are punished for making poor choices. In too many homes I see parents making far too much out of too little.

From page 104: I have used this entire chapter to demonstrate one thing—anything is easier than real discipline. It's much easier to be permissive and to just "let it go." And it is even easier to punish because you allow yourself the luxury of letting off steam and you usually don't have to follow through and make sure your child actually learns something.

✔ Reflect together

Discuss one or more of the following, as time permits:

1. What does it mean to "pull the rug out"? When have you seen this work in real life?
2. According to Dr. Leman, when is spanking appropriate and inappropriate? Talk about the right and wrong ways to spank. Which of these guidelines did you find most helpful?
3. How is it possible to "spank with love"?
4. Of the six ways to help your child feel loved, which do you hope to practice more skillfully—or frequently—in the days ahead?
5. What is the power behind giving children "the power of choice"? How could this work in your family?
6. Suggest some practical ways parents can earn their children's respect.
7. How did you like the story of Todd and his kitchen-sinked chicken dinner? How would this approach work in your home? Can you offer any of your own suggestions about how to handle a picky eater?
8. Is it true, as Dr. Leman says, that "anything is easier than real discipline"? Explain.
9. What other *insights* came to mind from this chapter? What new *questions* surfaced for you? Do you have any *personal applications* to consider? Explain.

Chapter Six

Danger—Super Parent at Work!

✔ Recall the chapter

- Choose a portion of this chapter that had particular impact on you. Tell other group members how this idea or issue "rang a bell" with you.
- What personal story or experience comes to mind in relation to these chapter themes: (1) *being a Super Parent,* or (2) *building a healthy family?* Talk about it!

✔ Respond to the text

How do you react to the text quotations below? For each, tell *how it applies*—or could apply—to your own family situation. If possible, offer a *personal example* from your experience with the issue.

> From page 117: Whenever I deal with a family who believes it has a "black sheep" child, I frequently ask the entire family to meet with me. It's important that the family see the misbehavior of one child not as just that child's problem. . . . Often the family members are contributing to what is going on.

> From page 121: Super Parents depend more on themselves than on God. They may talk about trusting God, but their parenting style reveals that their basic trust is in themselves. They seem to enjoy the role of judge and jury or answer man or lady. They push so hard for excellence that their children are frozen by fear of failure.

From page 123: There is nothing wrong with being human, but there is a great deal wrong with being hypocritical. I believe that when I freely admit my humanness to my children, I am taking advantage of an ideal opportunity to teach them dependence upon the grace of God.

✔ Reflect together

Discuss one or more of the following, as time permits:

1. How would you describe the Super Parent Syndrome? Tell about any ways you've suffered from this dreaded disease!
2. Review the four kinds of faulty reasoning that trap Super Parents. Which have plagued you the most? What advice does Dr. Leman offer to parents making each of these mistakes?
3. Why is it so tempting to try to "own" our children?
4. How would you have dealt with Ricky and Bobby at bedtime? In general, what does it take to stop playing judge-and-jury with our children?
5. Dr. Leman says that failure is good for children. Do you agree? When have you, as an adult, learned something crucial through your failure?
6. What are some likely results of trying to make all of your child's decisions? What is the alternative?
7. What was your reaction to the story of Super Mom Michelle? Do you have any similar tendencies as a mom or dad? If so, talk about a practical step you could take to "go on strike."
8. What other *insights* came to mind from this chapter? What new *questions* surfaced for you? Do you have any *personal applications* to consider? Explain.

Chapter Seven

The Way to Be Your Child's Best Friend

✔ Recall the chapter

- Choose a portion of this chapter that had particular impact on you. Tell other group members how this idea or issue "rang a bell" with you.
- What personal story or experience comes to mind in relation to this chapter theme of *being your child's best friend*? Talk about it!

✔ Respond to the text

How do you react to the text quotations below? For each, tell *how it applies*—or could apply—to your own family situation. If possible, offer a *personal example* from your experience with the issue.

From page 131: Some children reared in authoritarian homes remain "good little boys and girls" until they reach upper adolescence or early adulthood, and then they get their revenge through open rebellion, rejection of their faith, and so on. And I have counseled many adults who don't rebel until later in life. Many a "mid-life crisis" is a man or a woman working out feelings about an authoritarian upbringing.

From page 133: As you use natural or logical consequences with your child, be willing to explain things but don't go over and over the ground rules and don't give a lot of warnings, extra chances, and so on. One of your key goals is to teach your child that consequences in life are real and life doesn't always give a second chance.

From pages 134–35: Our children are so adept at holding us at bay and making us feel guilty. They have any number of ways of communicating to us that we have to warn them and cajole them and coax them and even bribe them. All of that is nonsense!

✔ Reflect together

Discuss one or more of the following, as time permits:

1. When have you been able to effectively communicate: "I love you, but I don't like what you did"? Why is this a difficult thing to do with our children?
2. What is the one basic question kids keep asking their parents? To what extent are *you* still asking it (whether or not your parents are still living)?
3. Describe the role of "balance" in reality discipline. Assess where you are, at the moment, on the "balance beam" between authoritarian and permissive parenting.
4. What does it mean to "always keep short accounts" with our children? Can you give a practical example?
5. How can remorse be a child's weapon? What can we do when that weapon is pointed at us? (Refer to the story of the nine-year-old daughter who left chores undone.)
6. Why is it so hard for us to accept dropping down on our child's "popularity list" when we stand firm for accountability? What helps you most when he or she starts piling on the guilt?
7. What other *insights* came to mind from this chapter? What new *questions* surfaced for you? Do you have any *personal applications* to consider? Explain.

Chapter Eight

When the Nuclear Family Explodes

✔ Recall the chapter

- Choose a portion of this chapter that had particular impact on you. Tell other group members how this idea or issue "rang a bell" with you.
- What personal story or experience comes to mind in relation to these chapter themes: (1) *being a single parent,* or (2) *supporting single parents?* Talk about it!

✔ Respond to the text

How do you react to the text quotations below? For each, tell *how it applies*—or could apply—to your own family situation. If possible, offer a *personal example* from your experience with the issue.

> From pages 142–43: In the first two years the pain will pop up in many surprising ways . . . . Sometimes your children will lash out in anger. If you're nearby, they will lash out at you. (That's the thing about anger; it's not always picky about its target.) Some children will close up, refusing to display emotion. Some will seem self-destructive. Some will stop working at school. Some will just refuse to do anything you ask.

> From page 147: Remember that your kid is just a kid. Many of your feelings are "adult" in nature—complex, conflicted. Your child isn't ready for all that. *You* may feel great after unburdening yourself to your listening child, but now

the child is bearing your burdens and may crumble underneath that load.

✔ Reflect together

Discuss one or more of the following, as time permits:

1. Dr. Leman says most single parents have to deal with an emotional stewpot that accompanies loss. Talk about the special emotional dynamics that pervade the single-parent household.
2. What things do you do to take care of yourself? How can you tell when you're not getting enough self-nurture? (Name some of your unique symptoms.)
3. Dr. Leman advises that we understand our children's pain while not indulging it. What does this mean to you in practical terms?
4. If you are a single parent, what do you think about the idea of "house rules"? Do you have them? If not, work with other group members to come up with a few you could try in the future.
5. What does it mean to avoid triangle relationships?
6. Where do you draw the line between having an older child help out with the younger ones . . . and making a co-parent out of him or her?
7. Review Dr. Leman's advice about a single parent's love life. What, in his comments, do you find most helpful?
8. What other *insights* came to mind from this chapter? What new *questions* surfaced for you? Do you have any *personal applications* to consider? Explain.

Chapter Nine

Families Don't Blend, They Collide

✔ Recall the chapter

- Choose a portion of this chapter that had particular impact on you. Tell other group members how this idea or issue "rang a bell" with you.
- What personal story or experience comes to mind in relation to these chapter themes: (1) *blending a family,* or (2) *dealing with family conflicts?* Talk about it!

✔ Respond to the text

How do you react to the text quotations below? For each, tell *how it applies*—or could apply—to your own family situation. If possible, offer a *personal example* from your experience with the issue.

> From page 158: The best way to win respect is to *give it.* Sometimes stepparents confess to me that they really don't love their spouse's children. Fine, I say. You don't have to love them, just respect them. At the very least they are human beings who live in your home. They are also the off-spring of the one you love. They have feelings and ideas and dreams and goals. The more you listen to them, the more you treat them with honor and respect, the safer they will feel with you. Eventually they will return that respect.

> From page 162: Again and again, I've heard about stepchildren's efforts to sabotage the new marriage. . . .

There are regular attempts to pose the question, "Who's more important: me or your spouse?"

You can fight and win these battles, but I think it's wiser to step out of the triangle. That is, find visible ways to support your spouse's relationship with his or her children. As the children realize it's not an either-or situation, they'll have less to fight about.

✔ Reflect together

Discuss one or more of the following, as time permits:

1. Review all of Dr. Leman's guidelines for family blending: Have each person choose one or more of the guidelines to describe and illustrate for the other participants.
2. Dr. Leman says that, at a wedding, at least six people are getting married. What does he mean?
3. Are you surprised by how long it usually takes to blend a family? In your experience or observation, what things make blending so difficult?
4. What does it mean to "compare rulebooks" in the blended family? How is this beneficial?
5. Why should we look for respect but not necessarily love from stepchildren?
6. What steps can be taken to help kids grieve for the lost past? Why is this often threatening or risky for the adults?
7. What kinds of "grenades" might an ex-spouse toss into the new family? Suggest some fictional explosive scenarios—then talk about possible responses and solutions in your group.
8. What other *insights* came to mind from this chapter? What new *questions* surfaced for you? Do you have any *personal applications* to consider? Explain.

Chapter Ten

How to Act When They Act Up

✔ Recall the chapter

- Choose a portion of this chapter that had particular impact on you. Tell other group members how this idea or issue "rang a bell" with you.
- What personal story or experience comes to mind in relation to this chapter theme: *dealing with a child's misbehaviors?*

✔ Respond to the text

How do you react to the text quotations below? For each, tell *how it applies*—or could apply—to your own family situation. If possible, offer a *personal example* from your experience with the issue.

From page 172: Every parent should be aware that *most* fears resulting in nightmares, night terrors, and abnormal thoughts and feelings are a direct result of allowing children to watch violence on television. . . . . Middle-class fathers of preschool children spent an average of thirty-seven seconds a day with their children—that's less than five minutes a week! In contrast . . . children watched television fifty-four hours per week!

From page 184: In every way possible, try to convey to your children at an early age that all parts of their bodies are good, wonderful, and given by God. Everything we are is part of God's plan for our lives. As your children get older (above six) you can start talking about the gift of sex and how Mommy and Daddy make babies.

From pages 186–87: [Parents] want their children to be able to challenge them and to say how they feel, but when they cross that unseen but very real line and become impudent, a little switch goes off inside a parent's brain. A little voice says, *You can't say that to me. Don't you know who I am? I'm your mother!*

✔ Reflect together

Discuss one or more of the following, as time permits:

1. Of the eleven behaviors dealt with in this chapter, which are most relevant to your situation these days? How have you been coping so far? What have you found particularly helpful in this chapter?
2. What does Dr. Leman mean by "getting behind your child's eyes"?
3. Dr. Leman says, "One of the best ways to help your children with their fears is to talk about your own fears." Do you agree? Talk about your own fears as a child. How did your parents respond? What helped you the most to grow out of your fears?
4. Why do siblings fight? Comment on some of the things Dr. Leman suggests we can do to prevent this.
5. What "payoffs" can a child receive from forgetting?
6. Talk about the "specialness" of mother-son and father-daughter relationships. What is the crucial attitude for parents in this relationship?
7. How do you handle tattling in your home? Is your method working? Talk about it!
8. What other *insights* came to mind from this chapter? What new *questions* surfaced for you? Do you have any *personal applications* to consider? Explain.

Chapter Eleven

The Daily Battle

✔ Recall the chapter

- Choose a portion of this chapter that had particular impact on you. Tell other group members how this idea or issue "rang a bell" with you.
- What personal story or experience comes to mind in relation to these chapter themes: (1) *dealing with the daily battles,* or (2) *learning strategies for conflict resolution with kids?* Talk about it!

✔ Respond to the text

How do you react to the text quotations below? For each, tell *how it applies*—or could apply—to your own family situation. If possible, offer a *personal example* from your experience with the issue.

From page 199: The statistics on children who are abused, used, kidnapped, and even killed are rising every year. This is reality and you should take the time to help them understand. You are not trying to frighten them but to make them wise.

From page 206: In order for parents to fulfill their mission, they must realize that their children want to belong. All children have two basic choices: They can identify themselves with their family or they can identify themselves with their peer group—the other kids on the block or at school. Rest assured, however, that your children will belong somewhere.

From page 209: It's not too hard to understand why a child gets these ideas of power. We really do act rather silly and say some silly things after a child has gone potty. Reinforce the child, yes; but to say, "Ohhhh, would you look at that!" or "Look at the pretty present Festus gave to Mommy," is really making far too much out of a basic act.

✔ Reflect together

Discuss one or more of the following, as time permits:

1. What is the typical bedtime routine with your child(ren)? How well is this working to circumvent bedtime battles?
2. How would the "penny game" work at your dinner table? If anyone has tried it—please report!
3. Dr. Leman says: "You can't make another person do anything." If this is true, what is reality discipline's basic alternative? Refer, for instance, to getting Buford up for school in the mornings.
4. Review the suggestions for handling homework problems. Discuss their potential effectiveness in your home.
5. Respond to Dr. Leman's suggestion for helping a child feel "I belong" in the family. Which would you, personally, like to focus on in the days ahead? Why?
6. Is the television a monster in your home? If so, assess the suggested steps to take. Do you have any additional ideas?
7. Talk about your worst and best travel experience, either in your current family or your family of origin when you were a child. What works best to keep "traveling terrors" at bay?
8. What other *insights* came to mind from this chapter? What new *questions* surfaced for you? Do you have any *personal applications* to consider? Explain.

Chapter Twelve

Winning Ways

✔ Recall the chapter

- Choose a portion of this chapter that had particular impact on you. Tell other group members how this idea or issue "rang a bell" with you.
- What personal story or experience comes to mind in relation to this chapter theme: *parenting strategies for applying reality discipline?* Talk about it!

✔ Respond to the text

How do you react to the text quotations below? For each, tell *how it applies*—or could apply—to your own family situation. If possible, offer a *personal example* from your experience with the issue.

From page 219: As you cultivate the skill of active listening, you will do less and less lecturing and giving of right answers. You will resist the temptation to try to readily solve all the problems in your child's life. And you will do more and more empathizing—letting your child know that you understand how he feels and that you care about his feelings.

From page 223: Never accept excuses. When you begin to accept the child's excuses, you are really tempting him to always point his finger in some other direction than at himself. You encourage him to always find the fault elsewhere and not to face his own responsibilities.

From page 226: Keep in mind that results aren't always evident over the short term. . . . If your child doesn't always respond to the techniques of reality discipline, don't give up. You are going to discipline your child in one way or another, regardless of the results, and you might as well be using a system that is based on Scripture (Eph. 6:4), which will pay off in the long run.

✔ Reflect together

Discuss one or more of the following, as time permits:

1. The first two steps when there's a problem are listen and respond to feelings. How good are you at these things? Can you share a recent example?
2. Why is it important to distinguish between getting angry at your child and getting angry at what your child does? How do "I" and "you" statements come into play here?
3. What are some critical differences between praising your child and giving her encouragement? How can praise actually be *discouraging*?
4. How easy or difficult is it for you to say "I love you" to your child(ren)? To your spouse? To yourself?
5. Dr. Leman says that reality discipline "cuts both ways." What does he mean? How does love play a role?
6. Review the guidelines for using "time out" with children. In your opinion, what are its pros and cons?
7. What other *insights* came to mind from this chapter? What new *questions* surfaced for you? Do you have any *personal applications* to consider? Explain.

Other Resources by Dr. Kevin Leman

Videos

How to Get Kids to Do What You Want
Living in a Stepfamily
Raising Successful and Confident Kids
Why Kids Misbehave
Parenting by Heart
Bringing Up Kids without Tearing Them Down
Becoming a Couple of Promise

realFAMILIES Video Club—Teaching tapes with Dr. Kevin Leman and Dr. Jay Passavant—call (877) 4REALUS for more information.

Poster

"A Child's Ten Commandments to Parents"

Audiotapes

Making Children Mind without Losing Yours
Sex Begins in the Kitchen
The Deception of Perfection
Raising Successful and Confident Kids
How to Get Kids to Do What You Want Them to Do
How to Be a Healthy Authority over Your Child
Why Kids Misbehave and What to Do about It
How to Make Your Child Feel Special
The Powerful Secrets of Reality Discipline
Keeping Your Family Together When the World Is Falling Apart
Living in a Stepfamily without Getting Stepped On

Dr. Kevin Leman, founder of Couples of Promise, is the author of twenty-one books on marriage and family. His books have sold millions of copies and include *The New Birth Order Book*, *Sex Begins in the Kitchen*, *When Your Best Is Not Good Enough*, *Bringing Up Kids without Tearing Them Down*, *Women Who Try Too Hard*, *Becoming a Couple of Promise*, and *What a Difference a Daddy Makes*.

A master communicator, Dr. Leman is an internationally known psychologist and humorist. He is also a regular guest on national radio and television talk shows, including *Focus on the Family with Dr. James Dobson*, *The View*, *Oprah*, *Live with Regis Philbin*, *CNN*, *The 700 Club*, *At Home—Live with Chuck and Jenni*, and *Today*. Dr. Leman has served as a consulting family psychologist for *Good Morning America*.

Dr. Leman attended North Park College and received his bachelor's degree in psychology from the University of Arizona, where he later earned his master's degree and doctorate. He and his wife, Sande, live in Tucson, Arizona. They have four daughters and one son.

For additional resources, or for seminar information, please contact:

Dr. Kevin Leman
Couples of Promise
P.O. Box 35370
Tucson, AZ 85704
Phone: (520) 797-3830
Fax: (520) 797-3809
web sites: www.realfamilies.com
www.couplesofpromise.com